Writing in the
Social Sciences

Writing in the Social Sciences

A GUIDE FOR TERM PAPERS AND BOOK REVIEWS

Jake Muller

OXFORD
UNIVERSITY PRESS

OXFORD
UNIVERSITY PRESS

8 Sampson Mews, Suite 204, Don Mills, Ontario M3C 0H5
www.oupcanada.com

Oxford University Press is a department of the University of Oxford.
It furthers the University's objective of excellence in research, scholarship,
and education by publishing worldwide in

Oxford   New York

Auckland   Cape Town   Dar es Salaam   Hong Kong   Karachi
Kuala Lumpur   Madrid   Melbourne   Mexico City   Nairobi
New Delhi   Shanghai   Taipei   Toronto

With offices in

Argentina   Austria   Brazil   Chile   Czech Republic   France   Greece
Guatemala   Hungary   Italy   Japan   Poland   Portugal   Singapore
South Korea   Switzerland   Thailand   Turkey   Ukraine   Vietnam

Oxford is a trade mark of Oxford University Press
in the UK and in certain other countries

Published in Canada
by Oxford University Press

Library and Archives Canada Cataloguing in Publication

Muller, Jake, 1947–
Writing in the social sciences : a guide for term papers and book reviews / Jake Muller.

Includes bibliographical references and index.
ISBN 978-0-19-543026-4

1. Social sciences—Authorship. 2. Report writing. 3. Book reviewing. I. Title.

PE1479.S62M85 2010   808'.0663   C2009-906131-7

Cover image: Sasha Martynchuk / iStockphoto

This book is printed on permanent (acid-free) paper ∞

Printed and bound in Canada.

2 3 4 — 13 12 11

MIX
Paper from
responsible sources
FSC   FSC® C004071
www.fsc.org

Table of Contents

Acknowledgements

There are many people that I would like to thank for helping to bring this book to fruition. At Oxford University Press, I am grateful to Katherine Skene for her interest in following up on my original book proposal; Ryan Chynces, Acquisitions Editor, for his support of this project; and Peter Chambers, Developmental Editor, for helping to create a better manuscript. The criticisms of the anonymous peer reviewers were greatly appreciated and were used to improve this book. I also wish to thank Colleen Ste Marie, who did the copy editing, as well as Ariel Bourbonnais, for her work as Production Coordinator.

I have benefited from many students, colleagues, and friends. While they are too numerous for me to mention individually, I would like to express my particular gratitude to Melissa Munn, University of Calgary, for her critical comments and support of this project. As well, I have benefited from many helpful discussions on writing with Eric Turner, who teaches physics and calculus at Northwest Community College.

Finally, I wish to thank my brother, Peter Muller, for his understanding of what was involved in creating this book. I likewise thank Barbara Hammer for her comments, sense of humour, and support throughout this project.

Jake Muller
Terrace, British Columbia
Canada

Introduction

Preparing for Your Social Science Term Paper and Book Review

This Introduction will present the following:

1. How this book will help you write a term paper or book review
2. Preliminary computer knowledge and skills that you will need
3. Basic knowledge and skills about reading and writing that you will need
4. Fundamental expectations about your new research and writing role
5. Specific requirements you will need to follow in your term paper

1. How Will This Book Help Me Write a Term Paper or Book Review?

The aim of this book is to help you, a beginning student, to research and write your first social science term paper or book review (and article critique) at a community college or university. You will find this book helpful if you are

- a first- or second-year social science student (for example, anthropology, psychology, sociology);
- a student in an applied or career program (for example, criminology, social or community services, teaching assistant); or
- a senior high school student preparing for social science courses.

Because you are just starting to learn material for your course(s), this book uses little specialized jargon from any discipline. The book is brief because it is a supplement (or complement) to the subject matter being taught. In fact, you can read and work on the book on your own.

What you will get from this book is guidance about the following:

- A beginning argumentative format and process for researching and writing a social science term paper or undertaking a book review (or article critique)
- Some ways to adapt this format and process to suit various social science instructors, each of whom may require you to write different kinds of argumentative term papers or book reviews (or article critiques)

- Some ways of adding to this beginning format for future term papers or book reviews
- Some common referencing styles to help you document your research sources in accordance with the *Publication Manual of the American Psychological Association* (APA) (2010, 6th edition)
- Ways this format and process can be used to evaluate and grade your term paper or book review (or article critique)

To write a *term paper* you should

- read this Introduction and make sure you understand it,
- skim through Chapters 1 to 5 to get an overview, and then
- work through Chapters 1 to 5.

To write a *book review* or *article critique* you should

- read this Introduction and make sure you understand it,
- skim through Chapters 1 to 6 to get an overview, and then
- work through Chapter 6 in detail.

(If there is something that you do not understand in Chapter 6, look it up in Chapters 1 to 5, where more information is presented.)

As a new student you will become part of the general social science community of researchers and writers. You will learn new responsibilities or a new role as you undertake this enterprise for your instructor.

The general word *instructor* is used throughout this book to refer to the person for whom you are writing your term paper or book review (or article critique). She or he may also be your professor, teacher, teaching assistant, or tutorial assistant.

2. What Preliminary Computer Knowledge and Skills Do I Need?

A social science term paper is written on a computer. You are expected to have access to and be familiar with the following:

- Internet browser—for example, Windows Internet Explorer, Mozilla Firefox
- Search engine—for example, Google, Bing
- Word-processing software—for example, Microsoft Word

In particular, you should have a competent working knowledge of word-processing software because you will be using it to create an outline for your term-paper (or book review or article critique).

In preparation for your term paper you should also buy a separate storage device for your computer, such as a USB flash drive. Use it to back up your files regularly.

Tips

This book provides links to Web sites that may change, be redirected, or be removed. Wherever possible, we will also present the name of the organization that maintains the site. You can use this name (for example, college, university, professional association, or organization) to locate the organization's general Web site. Once you have located it, you can then search for the new link or information you are seeking. As well, you can check out this book's Web site at Oxford University Press (http://www.oupcanada.com), where the links will be updated if they do change.

3. What Do I Need to Know about Reading and Writing, and What Skills Do I Need?

Your instructor will expect you to have the basic knowledge and skills of reading and writing that are vital for researching and writing a social science term paper or book review. You must be able to read efficiently *and* effectively. The ability to read efficiently is necessary to find information and material for your research. The ability to read effectively includes the following:

- Understanding what you are reading and looking up unfamiliar words
- Being able to critically evaluate what you are reading
- Knowing how you will use the information in your term paper

Efficient and effective reading, then, is a crucial part of being able to undertake research and writing.

In addition, you must know and be able to use basic writing skills to present your research. Having good writing skills means that you can express clearly what you wish to present so that your instructor can understand your writing. As well, you must write logically and coherently, arranging your ideas and material in a consistent sequence. Your instructor should be able to follow the organization of your writing.

The basic writing skills referred to above include the following:

- Spelling
- Grammar
- Punctuation
- Sentences
- Paragraphs

You should read through the following sections and determine if you are able to understand them. In particular, try to answer the questions that appear in each section (except the section on paragraphs). The answers are provided in Appendix A. If you have problems with these questions, you should brush up with the tips provided in Appendix B.

Spelling

You must be able to spell commonly used words and know how to use them correctly. Words that are considered common are those that are found in general-use dictionaries. You should thus obtain or have access to the following:

- A recent, university-level dictionary, such as *The Canadian Oxford Dictionary* or the *Gage Canadian Dictionary*
- A thesaurus—a book that contains a list of *synonyms* (meaning "similar") and *antonyms* (meaning "opposite")

You may be familiar with Web sites that allow you to look up the meaning of words and other aspects, for example, http://www.dictionary.com. Most of these free Internet dictionaries can be used for a quick check on the meaning of a word. However, these dictionaries may be out of date or may present US spellings only. For a quick set of multiple Web-based definitions, try the Google search engine by entering "define: <word you are looking up>", for example, "define: adolescent". This Google search will present you with a number of results pertaining to the meaning of *adolescent*.

Try looking up the following words in a dictionary:

- *teen* or *adolescent*
- *runaway*
- *alcohol*
- *abuse*

Some word-processing software allows you to select Canadian English spelling. You will need to turn this feature on. This will help to highlight some of the spelling differences between Canadian English and American English, such as *cheque* and *check*. Current computer spell-checkers have difficulty with the correct spelling of a word in the context of a sentence. For example, you must know the difference in spelling between *there* and *their* in a sentence.

Can you identify the following spelling errors in the context of the sentence?

1. The parents hid there alcohol from they're kids.
2. There teen did not no to phone home.

Grammar

Grammar refers to the ways in which words are used in sentences. Your instructor will understand what you are writing about only when you use correct grammar.

Can you identify the grammar mistakes in the following? Remember, the answers are in Appendix A and additional tips appear in Appendix B. Can you determine the singular and plural agreement errors?

3. A teen ran away from homes.
4. Many teens ran away from their home.

Can you identify the use of a singular verb for a whole group and a plural verb for a group acting individually?

5. The family are worried about their runaway teen.
6. The family is worried about its runaway teen.

Tips   Check out the on-line writing lab (OWL) for grammar at Purdue University: http://owl.english.purdue.edu/handouts/grammar/index.html

Can you correct the following unclear or vague pronoun reference?

7. The parents are going out drinking, partying, and staying out late. She doesn't like them.

How would you correct this sentence, which is not grammatically parallel?

8. She was lying, cheating, and had to steal to survive.

Punctuation

Punctuation refers to the use of conventional marks, such as a comma or a period, to make your writing clear. Your instructor will assume that you have a good command of proper punctuation.

Where would you use a comma in the following sentence?

9. A runaway teen may require food and shelter and clothing.

Where would you use a colon and quotation marks in the sentence below?

10. The detox worker stated the policy clearly, You must follow the rules of this clinic or you will not be allowed to stay.

The general rule for a beginning student is to keep the punctuation simple. This will be easier if you keep your sentences simple.

Sentences

You must be able to write *complete* sentences that have a subject and a verb. You should keep your sentences short when you first start to write a social science term paper. Short sentences will help you to avoid run-on sentences.

Can you reword the following sentence fragment into a complete sentence?

11. The runaway teen's family.

Can you reword this run-on sentence into a proper sentence?

12. She ran away from home and didn't know where she would live and what she would be doing.

Paragraphs

The last item of the required basic writing skills is paragraphs. To write in paragraphs means that you are able to write in separate but related sentences. These related sentences must include a beginning sentence, a middle sentence or sentences, and an end sentence to make a paragraph. Here are the main features that you must know:

- The first sentence of the paragraph is the *topic sentence*, which presents one main idea or point.

- The other sentences follow by clarifying the words of the topic sentence.
- A final sentence ends the clarification or provides a *transition* (connection) to the next paragraph.

Two common problems for beginning students are (1) paragraphs with too many points or (2) paragraphs that are one sentence. Both make it difficult for the reader to understand what the writer is presenting. Too many points or ideas in a paragraph can be resolved by using more paragraphs. Writing more sentences to clarify your point or idea can expand a vague one-sentence paragraph.

Here is the specific link to understanding paragraphs from Purdue University's OWL:
http://owl.english.purdue.edu/owl/resource/606/01/

This completes the list of basic writing skills that your instructor will assume that you have. If you had problems understanding these and found it difficult to answer the questions correctly, you are probably not ready to write a social science term paper or book review.

If you lack these skills, take an English writing course first to improve your ability to understand and write clearly. You do not want to put yourself in a situation where you are trying to learn basic writing skills while you are also struggling to understand the material of a social science course(s). You will feel overwhelmed.

Check out the writing and learning resources available on your college or university Web site. Many of these resources are also available through the library.

If you feel that you have a good understanding of these basic writing skills, you are ready to write a social science term paper or book review. Remember, though, that you must continue to develop your knowledge and skills of writing beyond the elementary ones presented here.

4. What Will My Instructor Expect from Me in My Research and Writing Role?

Your instructor will expect the following from you as you carry out your new research and writing role:

- You must understand and follow your instructor's directions.
- You must be an ethical author who will not plagiarize.
- You must learn proper referencing to avoid plagiarism.

If you do not meet these expectations, you will lose marks and possibly fail your assignment.

You Must Understand and Follow Your Instructor's Directions

It may seem obvious that your instructor will assume that you are following her or his directions in writing your term paper or book review. This means that you understand the instructions given to you and that you will carry them out to the best of your abilities. If you do not understand any aspect of the requirements, then the onus is on you to talk to or consult with your instructor.

Reminder
Your instructor's directions prevail in writing a term paper or book review (or article critique), even over this book!

You Must Be an Ethical Author Who Will Not Plagiarize

In carrying out these requirements, your instructor expects you to do your own work. What this means for you is this: *everything in your social science term paper, book review, or article critique will be considered your work unless you include a reference to someone else's work.*

You are the author of your term paper or book review (or article critique) and will receive credit for doing that work.

To conduct yourself ethically means that you will *not* commit the following:

- Copy part or all of another student's work
- Download, copy, and paste from the Internet
- Buy or pay someone else to write your term paper or book review
- Sell your term paper or book review

The above are all examples of *unethical conduct* in writing a term paper or book review. They are also examples of plagiarism. *Plagiarism* means that you are trying to take credit for someone else's work. You are also participating in plagiarism if you are helping someone else achieve credit for work that she or he did not do. All instructors consider plagiarism stealing or theft.

Reminder
Most institutions have strict disciplinary policies in response to plagiarism. Penalties may include a failing grade or a potential expulsion from the student's institution.

To avoid plagiarism and unethical conduct, you need to understand the distinction between a student who helps you by editing your work and one who rewrites part of it. A more advanced student can help you edit your work, which is called peer editing. *Peer editing* generally refers to the process whereby another student points out your specific writing errors in spelling, punctuation, grammar, and sentences. Knowing these errors is helpful to you in order to improve your writing.

However, you must make these corrections yourself. When you do so, you are conducting yourself ethically because you are doing your own work.

If someone else, such as a student or friend, rewrites any part of your work, such as a sentence or a paragraph, then that is not your work. You would be claiming credit for writing that you did not do and that is not yours. This is also considered plagiarism and is unethical. You must know and use this distinction whenever someone helps you with your work.

You Must Learn Proper Referencing to Avoid Plagiarism

For a social science term paper based on research, you are expected to include *references*. These reference sources are from other authors whose ideas and research you are using for the purpose of your term paper (or other work).

When you provide a reference source or document your research sources, your instructor will know that you are using someone else's ideas or information in your term paper and giving that author credit. *You are expected to do this*. Indeed, using and giving credit to sources that assist you demonstrates to your instructor that you have done a lot of work for your term paper.

You will, however, run into serious problems with your instructor if you do not follow the proper referencing of someone else's ideas or research in your term paper (or book review). Essentially, when you do *not* provide a reference for an idea or information that is not yours, you are saying that this is your idea or information. Remember, anything in your term paper (or book review or article critique) is considered your work by your instructor. When you do not document your reference sources, your instructor will assume that you are trying to take credit for someone else's work and she or he will accuse you of plagiarism. And many colleges and universities subscribe to software companies (for example, turnitin.com) that detect plagiarism and unethical work.

To avoid plagiarism you *must* provide references

- for someone else's words, ideas, or information;
- for quotes, paraphrasing, summary, or a condensed version of another author's work; and
- for following someone's structure, organization, theme, or paragraph.

In other words, when you use someone else's work (their words, ideas, or information)—even when you reword their work in your own words (by paraphrasing, summarizing, or condensing it)—you *must* provide a reference to that author(s). You must also include a reference if you follow the author's organization of her or his idea(s), even for a paragraph, to avoid committing plagiarism. If you have any doubts about what to do, talk to your instructor *before* you hand in your work.

Because your instructor will not accept ignorance of plagiarism as an acceptable excuse, you must learn how to avoid it. This book will help you to avoid plagiarism. It will show you how to reference properly according to the APA formatting styles. In addition, this book will show you how using an outline will help you to

- record every source in your outline, and
- keep track of your sources in one place.

5. What Specific Requirements Must I Follow in My Term Paper?

Your instructor will inform you about specific requirements for your term paper. (See Chapter 6 for requirements for book reviews and article critiques.)

Reminder
You must record and follow your instructor's requirements.

Instructors in the social sciences and related fields of study generally require students to follow certain formatting and referencing styles. Many follow the styles of the *Publication Manual of the American Psychological Association* (APA). These are used here.

Due Date

Your instructor will give you a deadline for handing in your term paper.

Reminder
It is your responsibility to meet deadlines. Make sure that you write down all due dates.

Some instructors impose penalties if you submit your work after the date it is due. If you have a problem with the deadline, you should see your instructor *before* your work is due.

Length

Your instructor may stipulate the required length of your social science term paper in the following ways:

- Number of pages (for example, 6–8 pages or 10–12 pages)
- Number of words (for example, 1200–1500 words or 2500 words)
- Number of arguments (for example, five arguments or eight arguments)

This book presents a social science term paper based on *arguments* (this will be clarified starting with the next chapter). You must present enough arguments within your term paper to fulfill your instructor's page or word requirement. As a beginning student you may not know how many arguments to include because there are various factors that will affect your term paper length, such as writing style and ability to clarify ideas.

Tips

Have *more* arguments than necessary to fulfill page or word requirements. It is easier to reduce arguments by keeping the most convincing ones than it is to search for more arguments later.

For most students, a short five-argument term paper may take anywhere from 6 to 10 pages while a longer eight-argument one usually takes 8 to 12 pages to complete. Again, there are various writing factors that influence the total number of pages or words.

Reminder

Note that the term paper length does *not* include the title page, the abstract, or the references pages.

Standard Outline

Most instructors strongly recommend that you create and use an outline to write your term paper. This book will help you use a standardized outline to write your first social science term paper. This involves the following:

- You should use or create a computer file of a standardized outline from Appendix C or D of this book to get started.
- You should use this outline not just as an exercise but also as a template for writing your term paper.
- You must change or adapt this standard outline as directed by your instructor.

You should also find out the following from your instructor:

- Is your outline to be handed in? If so, what is the due date?
- Is the outline to be attached to your term paper?

Title Page (APA Style)

Most instructors require a title page for a term paper.

Tips

The APA does not state specific requirements for the title page of a student's term paper. Consequently, many instructors *adapt* the APA styles to their specific teaching circumstances. You must determine your instructor's specific requirements and follow them.

Students are generally required to have some or all of the following items on a title page. For now, record (so that you will remember) which of the following are required to be on your title page (see Chapter 5 for examples):

- A manuscript page header
- The title of the term paper
- Your name

- Your student number
- The course name and number, and the section number
- Your instructor's name
- The name of your college or university
- The date (by which the term paper must be submitted)

If you are unsure about any of these requirements, talk to your instructor to clarify them.

Abstract (APA Style)

An *abstract* is a brief summary of your term paper on a separate page after the title page. Check to see if you are required to include one. If yes, then follow the APA style for length and format (presented in Chapter 5).

References (APA Style)

A *reference* refers to the research source that you consult and use in your term paper. Your instructor may require you to have the following:

- A minimum number of sources (books or periodicals) to use in writing your research term paper
- Acceptable kinds of sources (your sources should contain quality information and will most likely come from various fields of study, including the one you are studying)

If you have any doubts about the acceptability of a source (for instance, a Web-based source), consult your instructor *before* you write your term paper.

The *APA referencing style* refers to a particular way of formatting your sources inside and at the end of your term paper (see Chapter 3 for details). For instructors who require this style, you must learn it to reference or *document* the sources that you use in your writing. For a social science term paper, you must learn to find, use, and record references. This book will help you learn how to do this.

Computer software exists to help you with referencing your sources of research and formatting them correctly according to the APA style. Such software, including RefWorks, EndNote, and MyBib, is referred to generally as reference management software.

Tips   RefWorks offers tutorials where you can learn the basics of using this software: http://www.refworks.com/tutorial/

Many college and university libraries use referencing software. Check with your librarian to see if it is *up-to-date*.

Page Numbers

You may be required to number your pages in different ways. Here are three possibilities:

- Arabic numerals, starting with the title page, are used throughout the term paper (for example, the title page is 1, the abstract page is 2, and the text starts on page 3).
- Lower-case Roman numerals are used for the title page and the abstract (for example, the title page is i, the abstract page is ii), while the text of the term paper starts with Arabic number 3.
- Lower-case Roman numerals are used for the title page and the abstract (for example, the title page is i, the abstract page is ii), while the text of the term paper starts with Arabic number 1.

If your instructor does not specify how to number the pages of your term paper, you should clarify this requirement. Many instructors follow the third possibility, and this way is illustrated in Chapter 5.

Margins, Font Size, and Type

To ensure that all students meet the required length of the term paper given in terms of pages, your instructor will usually stipulate the margins, font size, and type required. The following are generally required:

- Margins: one inch
- Font size: 12 point
- Font type: Times New Roman

Clarify the acceptable font size and type with your instructor *before* writing your term paper or book review.

Lastly, once your instructor has stated the specific requirements for your term paper, book review, or article critique, your instructor will assume that you are now starting to work on it.

Tips

Start working on your term paper, book review, or article critique now!

Chapter Summary

How this book will help you write a term paper or book review:

- This book will introduce you to a beginning argumentative format and process for researching and writing a social science term paper, book review, or article critique.
- This book will teach you some ways to adapt this format and process for various instructors who may require a different kind of argumentative term paper, book review, or article critique.
- This book will present you with some ways to add to this starting format and process for future term papers, book reviews, or article critiques.
- This book will present some common APA referencing styles to document your research.
- This book will inform you of some ways that your instructor might use this basic argumentative format and process to evaluate and grade your term paper, book review, or article critique.

The preliminary computer knowledge and skills you will need:

- You must have access to or have a computer.
- You must know how to use an Internet browser, search engine, and word-processing software.
- You should buy and use a backup storage device for your term paper or book review files.

The basic knowledge about reading and writing and required skills you must have:

- You must know how to read to understand and critically evaluate information.
- You must have basic writing skills of spelling, grammar, punctuation, sentences, and paragraphs.
- You will have to decide if you have the basic reading and writing skills to research and write a social science term paper or book review.

The fundamental expectations about your new research and writing role:

- You must follow your instructor's directions for your term paper or book review over those of this book.
- You must be aware that everything you write in your term paper or book review is considered your work unless you reference it.

- You must provide a reference source for someone else's words, ideas, information, or how these materials are organized and presented by someone else.
- If you do not provide a required reference source for the preceding, your instructor will accuse you of plagiarism.
- You must conduct your research and writing ethically (do your own work, do not simply copy and paste material, do not buy or sell your work).

Specific requirements to record for your term paper:

- You must record the specific requirements for your term paper, including due date; length; standard outline; title page (APA style); abstract (APA style); references; page numbers; and margins, font size, and type. (See below.)

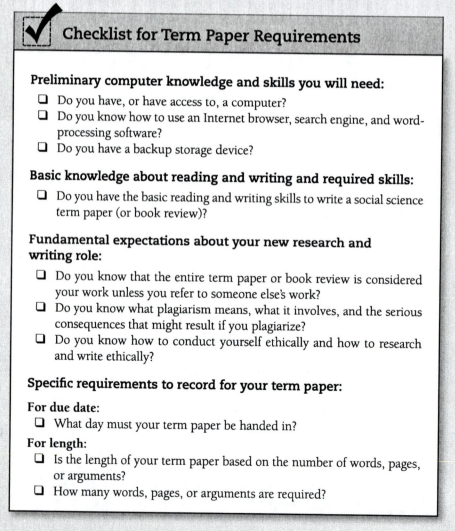

✓ Checklist for Term Paper Requirements

Preliminary computer knowledge and skills you will need:
- ❑ Do you have, or have access to, a computer?
- ❑ Do you know how to use an Internet browser, search engine, and word-processing software?
- ❑ Do you have a backup storage device?

Basic knowledge about reading and writing and required skills:
- ❑ Do you have the basic reading and writing skills to write a social science term paper (or book review)?

Fundamental expectations about your new research and writing role:
- ❑ Do you know that the entire term paper or book review is considered your work unless you refer to someone else's work?
- ❑ Do you know what plagiarism means, what it involves, and the serious consequences that might result if you plagiarize?
- ❑ Do you know how to conduct yourself ethically and how to research and write ethically?

Specific requirements to record for your term paper:

For due date:
- ❑ What day must your term paper be handed in?

For length:
- ❑ Is the length of your term paper based on the number of words, pages, or arguments?
- ❑ How many words, pages, or arguments are required?

For standard outline of term paper:
- ❑ Is a standard outline required as per Appendix C or D?
- ❑ Are any changes required to this standard outline as directed by your instructor?
- ❑ Does your outline have to be handed in?
- ❑ What is the outline due date, if the outline is required to be handed in?

For title page (APA style):
- ❑ Is a manuscript page header (APA style) required?
- ❑ Is an appropriate title required?
- ❑ Is your student name plus your number required?
- ❑ Is your course name and number plus section number required?
- ❑ Is your instructor's name required?
- ❑ Is your college or university name required?

For abstract (APA style):
- ❑ Is an abstract required for your term paper?

For references (APA style):
- ❑ What is the minimum number of references required?
- ❑ What are acceptable/unacceptable kinds of references?

For page numbering:
- ❑ Does your first page start with the title page?
- ❑ Does your first page start with the term paper (title page is not numbered)?

For margins, font size, and type:
- ❑ Does your paper have one-inch margins?
- ❑ What font size is required (for example, 12 point)?
- ❑ What font type is required (for example, Times New Roman)?

Recommended Web Sites

On writing and research from OWL at Purdue University:
http://owl.english.purdue.edu

On writing and research from the Writing Center at The University of Wisconsin at Madison:
http://www.wisc.edu/writing/Handbook/index.html

Recommended Readings

On details of the writing process and different kinds of writing:

Barnet, S., Stubbs, M., Bellanca, P., & Stimpson, P.G. (2003). *The practical guide to writing*. Toronto: Pearson.

Hacker, D. (2006). *The Bedford handbook*. (7th ed.). Boston: Bedford/St. Martin's.

Norton, S., & Green, B. (2006). *Essay essentials*. (4th ed.). Scarborough, ON: Thomson/Nelson.

On research and writing:

Lester, J.D., Lester, J.D. Jr., & Mochnacz, P.I. (2003). *The essential guide to writing research papers*. Toronto: Longman.

Northey, M. (2007). *Making sense: A student's guide to research and writing*. (5th ed.). Don Mills, ON: Oxford University Press.

Chapter 1

Learning the Basic Social Science Argumentative Format and Process

To start you on your way to research and write a social science term paper, you will need to learn the following:

1. The basic social science argumentative format and process
2. The argumentative roots of the basic social science argumentative format and process
3. How to choose one of three kinds of term papers
4. How to use a standardized social science outline for your research priorities and for writing your term paper
5. How to visualize the research and writing process

1.1 What Is the Basic Social Science Argumentative Format and Process?

A basic social science argumentative format and process for writing a term paper (or a book review or an article critique) is presented below (notably 1 to 5). This is followed by the meaning of these words or *terms*. The APA style is the required format for in-text citations and for the references page.

The Basic Social Science Argumentative Format and Process
1. Aim
2. Definition of concepts
3. Organization of arguments
4. Presentation of arguments
5. Conclusion
6. In-text citations (APA style)
7. References (APA style)

All seven of these items are elaborated on in future chapters (especially in Chapters 2 to 4).

Tips | Remember the terms in the box above and their general meaning.

Here is the general meaning of the terms in the box above:

- *Aim*: The word *aim* is used to refer to the overall purpose or focus of the term paper. For a beginning student, the aim of the term paper should be written in a sentence. Hence, the aim sentence states the overall purpose and guides your entire term paper.
- *Definition of concepts*: The aim sentence will contain key ideas or concepts. These ideas or concepts are defined so the reader will be able to understand their meaning and use. *Definition of concepts* thus refers to clarifying the meaning of the words that present these key ideas, thoughts, or mental images. The meaning or definition of these concepts in your aim is used for your entire term paper.
- *Organization of arguments*: This refers to the sequence or order of arguments. Your term paper will contain arguments that are arranged in a logical manner to support an aim.
- *Presentation of arguments* (or simply *arguments*): The word *argument* includes two parts—point and evidence. The word *point* refers to the reason for presenting your argument, concerning your aim. The point of the argument is the idea that is being put forward. The *evidence* is the information, fact, result, or example that is used to substantiate the point. An argument must consist of a point and the evidence to support that point in order to be called an argument. An argument is used to uphold or substantiate the aim sentence or, simply, the aim.
- *Conclusion*: This refers to the summary and end of the term paper. Your social science term paper must have a conclusion.
- *In-text citations*: These refer to the research sources within the term paper. The in-text citations are those sources used in your term paper and formatted according to the APA style.
- *References*: This refers to the full text of all your research sources that are used in your term paper and formatted according to the required APA style. The references page is the last part of your term paper and thus appears at the end of your paper.

Here is some clarification of the terms *social science*, *format,* and *process* in the phrase "basic social science argumentative format and process."

- *Social science*: This term is used here in its widest meaning to include all the disciplines or fields (and related applied fields) that study people (behaviour, social interactions, and groups) in society. Other possible terms could be *behavioural science* or *life science*.
- *Format*: This refers to the individual items or parts in our list on p. 17. The word *basic* in this format means that these items are the minimum number that must be used. To use the basic social science argumentative format to research and write a term paper, then, means that you must include all seven items.

- *Process*: The word *process* is used in two general ways: (1) the writing process and (2) the research process. In the writing process, *process* refers to the sequence of writing the items or parts in the social science format. In the research process, *process* refers to the sequence of research. The research process is divided into first and second priorities. The first priority process starts the research, and the second one ends it.

All the items in the basic social science argumentative format and process are used in the outline for your term paper.

1.2 What Are the Argumentative Roots of the Basic Social Science Argumentative Format and Process?

The basic social science argumentative format and process is part of a *general argumentative tradition* of research and essay writing. Writers and researchers have carried on this argumentative research tradition or rhetoric tradition for centuries (Booth, Colomb, & Williams, 2008, pp. 9–15). The basic social science format and process is part of this larger argumentative community. Knowing how the social science argumentative format and process relates to the argumentative tradition will show you

- that the starting items (the words and phrases) of the basic social science argumentative format and process come from the earlier, argumentative tradition (Corbett & Connors, 1999) and that they are not unique or original; they are a basic part (a start or foundation) of more aspects in the argumentative tradition;
- that the items in the basic social science argumentative format and process are similar (despite using some different words) to those of the argumentative essay;
- how much of an argumentative essay you are starting with by using the basic social science argumentative format and process; and
- that you still need to learn from the argumentative tradition to write a more convincing term paper (or book review or article critique).

The argumentative research tradition and basic social science argumentative format and process for writing a term paper are essentially similar. The two main differences are as follows:

1. The traditional argumentative essay has reasons and evidence to support a thesis or a claim that states the overall argument presented. The basic social science argumentative format and process has points (or reasons) and evidence as arguments to support an aim (or thesis).
2. The basic social science format and process for writing a term paper starts with fewer parts or items than the traditional argumentative essay.

In the general argumentative tradition, the overall essay or term paper is referred to as an *argument*. The author's overall argument consists of a *claim* or a position taken on an issue. This claim or position is supported by reasons and evidence to make the claim convincing (Wood, 2001, p. 6). A claim may also be called a *thesis* (Wood, 2001, p. 127). The thesis statement or claim refers to the sentence in which the author presents a stance or position on a topic or issue. The thesis statement is the overall argumentative position that the author will try to persuade the reader to accept.

The basic social science format and process for a term paper also has a general stance or position that is stated in the *aim* sentence. The aim is similar to a thesis and claim since all refer to the position that an author takes on a topic or issue. One difference between these two approaches, however, is in the use of the word *argument*. In the basic format and process, the word *argument* is limited to points and evidence. Such a use of *argument* would only refer to the reasons and evidence in the general argumentative tradition and not to a general use to refer to the overall argument being advanced. Hence, the word *argument* is used in a specified way in the basic format and process to help students learn the starting features for creating a generalized argument. As students become more experienced in creating and using arguments, they should be able to state that the general argument they are advancing is expressed in the aim sentence (as is the case in the general argumentative essay).

Furthermore, an argumentative research essay uses "information and analysis to support a thesis, to argue for a claim" (Seyler, 1999, p. 6). Research is undertaken to provide *reasons* and *evidence* to make a claim convincing (Wood, 2001, p. 6). Essentially, the claim or thesis of the essay is supported by reasons and analysis that are based on information and evidence.

The basic social science argumentative format and process is slightly different in its use of words to support an aim. The word *argument* is used to support the aim. An argument consists of points and evidence. The meaning of *point* includes "reason." The meaning of *evidence* to support points or reasons is identical for both approaches. So, for the basic format and process, an argument consists of a point and evidence to support an aim. In the argumentative research essay, the emphasis is on reasons and evidence to support a thesis or claim. The difference between the two approaches is that the word *argument* is used in the basic format and process to get students started and used to thinking that they are presenting arguments to support an aim (or thesis).

In addition, the basic social science argumentative format and process consists of fewer parts than the general argumentative tradition. A typical argumentative research essay, according to Kirszner and Mandell (2004), begins with an introduction that contains a thesis statement on a particular issue. The body presents the reasons and evidence that support the thesis (*inductively*, i.e., from specific reasons and evidence to a general thesis; or *deductively*, i.e., from a general thesis to specific reasons and evidence). As well, arguments against the thesis and a rejection of those arguments are also presented. The conclusion restates the thesis, but is worded differently, and includes a strongly worded closing statement (p. 544).

A term paper that is written by following the basic social science argumentative format and process has an introduction that includes an aim sentence (or thesis) on an issue or topic. Unlike the argumentative research essay, the introduction also includes defining concepts in the aim sentence and states how the arguments are organized to demonstrate the aim. Initially, the aim is developed from arguments (using *inductive* reasoning). *Deductive* reasoning is added later. The first kind of argument is usually limited to those that support the aim. Arguments that oppose the aim, and their rejection, are added later. The conclusion restates the aim sentence, summarizes the arguments, and clarifies how the arguments supported the aim. Unlike an argumentative research essay, there is no strongly worded closing statement.

The table below summarizes the relationship between these two approaches:

Argumentative Research Tradition	Basic Social Science Argumentative Format & Process
Introduction • Introduce the issue. • Provide thesis statement.	Introduction • Introduce the aim. • Provide aim sentence. • Define concepts. • Organize arguments.
Body • Use inductive reasoning: evidence to support the thesis. • Use deductive reasoning: thesis that requires supporting evidence. • State arguments against thesis and refute them.	Body • Use arguments to create aim (inductive). • Later, add arguments against aim and refute those arguments. • Later, add deductive reasoning.
Conclusion • Restate thesis. • Add a strongly worded closing statement.	Conclusion • Restate aim. • Restate arguments and how they supported aim.

As the table highlights, the basic social science argumentative format and process is a starting point for you to learn the argumentative research style:

- In the basic format and process, you expand the introduction to include the aim sentence (thesis statement), define the concepts in the aim sentence, and state how the arguments have been organized.
- You limit the argument section of the basic format and process to inductive reasoning until you become more familiar with making arguments and creating an aim sentence. Once you become comfortable with this, and gain more experience, you can then add deductive reasoning.
- As well, you must learn to add, to the basic format and process, arguments against your thesis or aim and provide reasons for rejecting those arguments. Indeed, your term paper may not be considered an argumentative research essay until you include these.
- Like the argumentative research essay, your conclusion in the basic format and process also focuses on restating the aim. However, in the basic format and process, you are also required to restate your arguments and how each supported your aim sentence.

On the whole, the basic social science argumentative format and process is a starting foundation for writing an argumentative research term paper. Because the basic format and process is similar to the argumentative research essay, you are able to do the following:

- Look for and recognize the words or similar ones (and their meaning) from the basic format and process in the research of other writers. Knowing to look for and to recognize, for example, an aim in a book, periodical, and on-line source will help you be more efficient in your research.
- Write your views and research in a factual manner. This point is best expressed by Booth et al. (2008). Their view is that you should write your essay or term paper as if you, along with your reader, were seeking a co-operative answer to an issue or question (p. 106). Thus, the tone of your argumentative term paper should be friendly and neutral, not antagonistic or coercive.

Tips Once you have learned the items of the basic format and process, see if you can find them in your textbook or readings. Check to see how they are used and what more you can learn about their use in your field of studies.

Some writers on argumentative essays encourage you to develop an outline from your research notes (Barnet & Bedau, 2002, pp. 233–234). However, as a beginning student you may have difficulty creating your first outline. You are just learning to construct convincing arguments that support an aim and need an outline format that emphasizes arguments. Therefore, creating your own outline may be quite unfamiliar to you.

A standard social science outline was created to help you get started. All parts of the basic social science argumentative format and process are included in the outline. Here are some benefits to using a common outline in starting your research:

- There is one place (or file) to record your arguments and all other aspects of your term paper (or book review or article critique).
- The outline allows you to keep track of your arguments (points and evidence) and note where more research may be needed.
- The research information within the outline can easily be revised and reorganized.
- Your research is already recorded and organized based on the way that your term paper will be written, so you will be in good shape to start writing it.

After you have gained some experience using a common outline (such as those in Appendix C or D), you are expected to develop your own for a term paper (or for a book review or article critique).

Before you start your research, you need to consider which one of three general kinds of term papers to write. The basic social science argumentative format and process is used to show you the research and writing that is involved in each one of these term papers.

1.3 How Do I Choose One of the Three Kinds of Term Papers?

You will need to decide which *one* of three kinds of term papers you plan to write. These three general kinds are as follows:

a. All the arguments are advanced to support the aim.
b. A majority of arguments support the aim while a minority oppose it.
c. There is a balance of arguments equally supporting and opposing the aim (the point and counterpoint type of essay).

Tips

If you are unsure what kind of term paper your instructor requires, read these three kinds to understand them. Decide *after* reading them which one or which variation of which kind is required. If you are unsure, consult your instructor right away.

A. All Arguments Support the Aim

Some instructors may begin by asking you to write a short argumentative term paper with a small number of arguments, such as up to five arguments. The reasons for such a short term paper may be as follows:

- To learn the various parts of the social science format
- To focus more on creating convincing arguments
- To practise writing this kind of a research term paper

Beginning social science students should know how to write such a starting term paper. The basic social science argumentative format and process is repeated here to show you the general requirements for this kind of term paper.

- *Aim*: You must have a properly worded aim. It may be a sentence or a question to be answered. The aim must be worded to suit your course, discipline, or field of studies.
- *Definition of concepts in the aim*: The concepts in your aim will normally be defined according to your course, discipline, or field of studies. You must find and use these definitions accordingly.
- *Organization of arguments*: You must arrange your arguments that support your aim in a sequence, from first to last.
- *Presentation of arguments*: Your instructor may specify the number of arguments that you are required to have in support of your aim. A short paper may have up to five arguments while a longer paper may have up to eight. You must fulfill this requirement. For each argument, you must present a point and evidence to support that point, and each argument must be worded clearly to relate to your aim.

If your instructor does not specify the number of arguments but states the number of words or pages, then you must have enough arguments to fulfill that requirement.

- *Conclusion*: Your conclusion must state how each of your arguments supported the aim.
- *References*: You must use the minimum number of references, as required by your instructor, in your term paper. Some instructors require fewer references for the first social science term paper (about six) and more for the second one (ten to twelve). Although these are a minimum, having a few more than the required number is preferable.

A longer term paper that has more arguments and references will result in a greater understanding of the material.

B. Majority of Arguments Support Aim While Minority Oppose It

For this kind of a term paper, the majority of arguments support the aim sentence. A minority of arguments, usually one or two, then oppose or contradict the aim. Each argument that opposes the aim is in turn argued against, or refuted, to show that the opposing argument has little or a negligible effect on the aim. You should refute each opposing argument after it is presented. In other words, state that the argument has minimal impact on the aim and give a specific reason for rejecting it.

This term paper begins in a similar way to the previous one. The requirements for the *aim* and *definition of concepts in the aim* are the same. Some differences start, however, with organization of arguments.

- *Organization of arguments*: The arguments (or arguments grouped into headings or themes) that support the aim are presented first. Arrange their sequence the same way as in the previous kind of term paper and state the arguments in general terms.

    As mentioned, follow this with a brief reference to the arguments opposed to the aim sentence. State these arguments and provide a general reason or reasons why they have a minimal or negligible effect on the strength of the aim sentence.
- *Presentation of arguments*: Present a majority of arguments in support of the aim. For example, for a five-argument term paper, you could present three to four arguments in support of the aim and one to two arguments in opposition to it.

    A reason(s) for rejecting an opposing argument may or may not be presented as an argument. If you present the reason for rejecting an opposing argument as an argument, then you will tend to be more convincing. A reason that you present as an argument should count as one of the total arguments required for an argumentative term paper. If, however, your stated reason is an incomplete argument, it should not count as one of your arguments.
- *Conclusion*: Begin your conclusion by restating the aim. Then, write a short sentence or two for each argument or group of arguments, stating how they supported the aim sentence. Follow with the arguments that oppose the aim.

You might conclude this kind of a term paper with a statement to the effect that there were valid arguments that opposed your aim. However, their impact was negligible, and most of the arguments clearly supported the aim.

- *References*: You will need more references for this type of term paper than for the previous kind. This is because introducing opposing arguments and then refuting them generally requires providing reference sources for them.

C. A Balance of Arguments Supports and Opposes the Aim

The final kind of social science term paper presented here is one where there is a balance of arguments between those that support an aim and those that oppose it. This kind of term paper can also be seen as presenting both sides of an issue or problem.

Before starting this kind of term paper, you must find out

- if your instructor expects you to remain *neutral* in presenting both sides of an issue, or
- if you are expected to take a position and present both sides.

Most instructors prefer you to choose one side of arguments over the other. Depending on your instructor's requirements, there are three different ways to construct this kind of term paper:

1. Start with a neutral aim sentence or pose a neutral question, present both sides of it, and make a neutral conclusion. This shows the instructor that you have a good grasp of both sides of an issue. You also demonstrate your ability to remain neutral on the issue.
2. Start from a neutral standpoint, examine both sides, and then state in the conclusion which side you are taking on the aim or question. In this kind of a term paper, you can show not only a good grasp of both sides of an issue but go one step further by deciding that one side of the arguments is more persuasive than the other.
3. Present an issue, point out that there are two sides to that issue, and state your position on it. In other words, you state your position clearly at the beginning of the term paper, present both sides of the issue, and then affirm your final stance in the conclusion. Although this kind of a term paper is similar to the previous one, the difference is that the side you take is stated at the outset.

Become familiar with how you take a stance in these three types of term papers, the major part of which is to present both sides of an issue. Decide which way your instructor wants you to set up your term paper. Since all three are related, learn to shift from one to another.

- *Aim*: Word your aim sentence as neutrally as possible. At this point, each one of the three ways will create a different term paper.

    In the first way, or neutral stand, add that the objective is to present both sides of the issue so that the reader can decide which side to take.

In the second way, after both sides have been presented fairly, suggest that one side will be favoured because of the persuasiveness of the arguments.

In the third way, state that although both sides will be presented, you clearly prefer one.

- *Definition of concepts in the aim*: Define the concepts in the aim sentence, whether written as an issue or as a question. Define those concepts in a convincingly neutral manner that does not favour one side over the other, thereby demonstrating to your instructor your ability to remain neutral.

If the favoured side uses a recognized concept from the course (or from the discipline or field of studies), then you will need to define that concept as well. However, if the side you choose uses everyday language, this is not necessary.

- *Organization of arguments*: There are two ways for you to organize your arguments. They are as follows:
  1. *Separate the supporting and opposing arguments.*   This is referred to as the *block method* (Stewart & Allen, 2005, pp. 107–108). Present all the arguments of one side followed by those of the other side. Unless directed by your instructor, decide for yourself which side to present first. You can start by presenting the arguments that oppose the issue followed by those that support it, or vice versa. However, write both sides of the issue *convincingly*. For the opposing arguments (grouped into headings or themes), follow the pattern of presenting the least important group of arguments first and end with the most important one. Use this pattern with the supporting groups of arguments as well.
  2. *Integrate the supporting and opposing arguments to show the preference for one side over the other.*   This is referred to as the *point-by-point method* (Stewart & Allen, 2005, pp. 109–110). For the *point-by-point method*—integrating the supporting and opposing arguments—show your preference for one side over the other. As in the first way, you can start with either supporting or opposing arguments. Continue to present one argument (or groups of arguments as headings or themes) advocating one side of the issue (the opposing side) followed by an argument for the supporting side throughout the paper. For separate arguments, start with the opposing arguments and then present the supporting side. You can do likewise with integrating the opposing and supporting sides of arguments. A reason for starting with arguments that you oppose is that you can then refute them with counter-arguments with which you agree.

     Although there are two general ways to present arguments (separated and integrated), try to use the integrated way in your paper in order to demonstrate a more knowledgeable, convincing understanding and analysis of the issue.

- *Presentation of arguments*: Present an equal number of arguments for and against an issue. For a five-argument term paper, this would mean presenting two arguments in support of the aim and two arguments opposed to it. One argument could then present the reason for favouring one side over the other.
- *Conclusion*: You can have three possible conclusions for a balance-of-arguments paper based on your aim.

1. In the first way, you can remain neutral and offer no opinion about either side of the issue. Typically, you can leave it up to the reader (in this case, your instructor) to decide which side is more convincing. The main emphasis in your paper has been on presenting arguments on both sides of the debate with a minimum of bias toward either side. An instructor who requires this kind of a term paper is interested in determining your ability to remain neutral on an issue or problem.

2. You can arrive at the second way to conclude after starting with a neutral stance in the aim sentence, presenting both sides, and then stating which side you favour. Provide a reason for preferring one side over the other. Typically, you would do this by finishing the statement, "This side was more convincing because . . ."

3. The third and final way for you to conclude this kind of a term paper is to reaffirm the side that you supported at the start. In other words, restate the side that you supported in the aim sentence (issue or problem). You still present arguments for both sides, but the arguments you favoured refute those that you opposed. Hence, in the conclusion you reaffirm the position that you supported at the outset of the term paper, based on the persuasiveness of those arguments.

- *References*: Just as with the previous kind of term paper, more references are required here for the same reason (i.e., because introducing opposing arguments and then refuting them generally requires providing reference sources for them).

This section has presented three general kinds of argumentative term papers for you to consider writing. There are many other kinds of essays that can be written in the argumentative tradition as Wood (2001) points out, such as Toulmin (pp. 122–140) or Rogerian (pp. 344–351). These are additional forms of argumentative essays that you will need to attempt. The basic social science argumentative format, however, should provide you with an excellent starting point for your further development.

Here are some further suggestions to help you decide which kind of term paper to write:

- If your instructor directs you to write a certain kind of essay, then you must do that. Use the basic social science argumentative format and process to help you.

- If your instructor gives you no direction, then she or he is most likely expecting type (b) (where a majority of arguments support the aim and a minority oppose it).

- If you have considerable writing experience (for example, you are an advanced student taking an introductory social science course) you might try (c) (where a balance of arguments equally supports and opposes an aim).

1.4 How Do I Use a Standard Social Science Outline for My Research Priorities and to Write My Term Paper?

There are three general steps involved in the overall process of writing your term paper:

- Create your outline.
- Work on research priorities and record all aspects in your outline.
- Write your term paper based on your completed outline.

Create Your Outline

- Create and use a computer file of one of the standard example outlines provided in Appendix C or D. (You might omit any unnecessary formatting, such as page or line borders.)
- Include all parts of the standard outline: from the title page to the references page. Leave some space to complete each section.
- Be sure to include all headings and subheadings in the outline that you create (for example, for Arguments section include point and evidence for each argument in your outline).
- You can also print your outline and take it with you to do research. Remember to record your research in your computer file outline.

Work on Research Priorities and Record All Aspects in Your Outline

- The basic social science argumentative format and process is separated into two related parts referred to simply as the first-priority items and the second-priority ones.
- The first-priority and second-priority items are listed below.

Research Priorities

First Priority:
- Aim
- Presentation of arguments
- In-text citations
- References

Second Priority:
- Definition of concepts
- Organization of arguments
- Conclusion
- In-text citations
- References

- Start your research with the first-priority items and record them in your outline until you have completed them (details in Chapters 2 and 3).
- Make any changes in the first-priority items as your research progresses.
- Revise your first-priority items before you start your second-priority ones.
- Research your second-priority items, record the research in your outline, and complete these items. Make any changes as necessary (details in Chapter 4).
- Once the second-priority items are finished, your outline is complete.

Some advantages to working with research priorities include the following:

- You can start working on parts of your term paper right away as you read or are being taught the chapters (these research priorities also form the basis for the way this book is organized).
- It is easy to make changes to the first priorities as you get started because you do not yet have to be concerned with the second ones.
- The first-priority items determine specifically what you will need to do for your second-priority items.
- Completing the first-priority items lessens the likelihood of making changes to your second-priority aspects.

In general, using research priorities from the basic social science argumentative format and process is a relatively efficient and effective way to complete your outline and then write your term paper.

Write Your Term Paper Based on Your Completed Outline

- You should plan on two general steps to write your term paper: (1) write a *draft* and then (2) *revise* your draft (details in Chapter 5).
- The completed outline gives you the main parts and the sequence to write a rough draft for your term paper.
- Here is the list of items to write your draft with an added introduction to arouse interest in your aim.

Writing the Term Paper Draft

(*Introduction to aim*) The (subject area/topic/issue) is important because . . .
(*Aim*) The aim of this paper is to demonstrate . . .
(*Definition of concepts*) The concepts in the aim that will be defined are . . .
(*Organization of arguments*) The sequence of the arguments will be as follows . . .
(*Presentation of arguments*) The first argument to demonstrate the aim (restate aim) is . . .
(*Conclusion*) In conclusion, this paper has demonstrated that (restate aim) . . .
(*In-text citations*) In APA style throughout term paper.
(*References*) In APA style.

- All parts of your written draft must be related through the use of *transitions* that connect your sentences, paragraphs, and ideas (see suggestions in Chapter 5).

- Once you have written a draft, revise it to make sure that it is complete, coherent, and unified, without basic writing errors.
- After you have revised your draft, complete the other parts, including proper formatting, the abstract (if required), and the title page.
- Completing all these parts will create your final copy, which you hand in to your instructor.

1.5 How Can I Visualize the Basic Social Science Research and Writing Process?

Two general diagrams are presented here to assist you with visualizing the basic social science research and writing process. The first diagram is a table that helps you to visualize

- knowing the basic social science argumentative format and process,
- working on the research priorities using a standard outline, and
- writing the social science term paper.

Know the basic social science argumentative format & process	Work on research priorities, using standard outline	Write the social science term paper

1. Aim
2. Definition of concepts
3. Organization of arguments
4. Presentation of arguments
5. Conclusion
6. In-text citations (APA style)
7. References (APA style)
	First Priority:
	  Aim
	  Presentation of arguments
	  In-text citations
	  References
	
	Second Priority:
	  Definition of concepts
	  Organization of arguments
	  Conclusion
	  In-text citations
	  References
		Introduction to aim
		Aim
		Definition of concepts
		Organization of arguments
		Presentation of arguments
		Conclusion
		(In-text citations, APA style)
		  throughout term paper)
		References (APA style)

As well, a general diagram, like a flow chart, is presented to help you visualize the various steps that are involved in order to research and write your term paper. This chart helps you to

- plan the sequence of your research and writing and
- keep track of where you are and what you need to do.

As you gain more experience through course work, research and writing is not as straightforward as it appears in these beginning diagrams. You may change one part, which will involve returning to another, and so forth. That is the nature of the creative process in research and writing. The diagrams, with their basic parts and steps, will help you start that journey.

A Basic Social Science Research and Writing Process

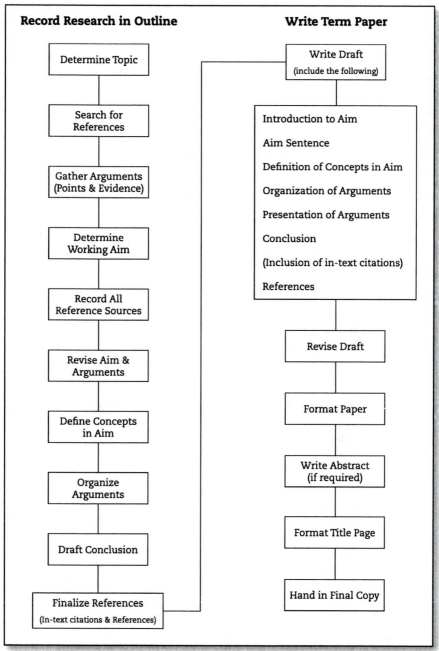

Record Research in Outline

- Determine Topic
- Search for References
- Gather Arguments (Points & Evidence)
- Determine Working Aim
- Record All Reference Sources
- Revise Aim & Arguments
- Define Concepts in Aim
- Organize Arguments
- Draft Conclusion
- Finalize References (In-text citations & References)

Write Term Paper

- Write Draft (include the following)
  - Introduction to Aim
  - Aim Sentence
  - Definition of Concepts in Aim
  - Organization of Arguments
  - Presentation of Arguments
  - Conclusion
  - (Inclusion of in-text citations)
  - References
- Revise Draft
- Format Paper
- Write Abstract (if required)
- Format Title Page
- Hand in Final Copy

Reminder

Start working on priority-one items now—research to create an aim and arguments and required reference sources.

Chapter Summary

Know the basic social science argumentative format and process:

- Include the aim, definition of concepts, organization of arguments, presentation of arguments, conclusion, in-text citations, and references.

Know what to add to the basic social science argumentative format and process from the argumentative research essay:

- Introduction to aim
- Aim
- Definition of concepts in aim
- Organization of arguments
- Presentation of arguments—inductive reasoning
- Conclusion

Add the following in future writings from argumentative research essay:

- Presentation of arguments—deductive reasoning
- Presentation of arguments against thesis and reasons for rejecting them

Consider writing one of three kinds of term papers:

a. Where all arguments support aim
b. Where a majority of arguments support aim while a minority oppose it
c. Where there is a balance of arguments

Use a standard social science outline for research priorities and for writing your term paper:

Create social science outline.

- Use or create a computer file of a standardized outline from Appendix C or D.
- Include all headings and subheadings.

Work on research priorities to complete outline.

- Start and complete first-priority items.
- Then complete second-priority ones to finish outline.

Write term paper based on completed outline.

- Use completed outline to write a draft of your term paper, with transitions.
- Revise draft (that is, proofread, check for coherence).
- Format term paper.
- Write abstract (if required).
- Include title page.

Visualize your research and writing:

- Use diagrams to plan your research and writing.
- Use chart of research and writing to check where you are in the process and to see what still needs to be completed.

 Checklist for Term Paper Research and Writing

Do you know the basic social science argumentative format and process?

Do you know what to add to the basic social science argumentative format and process from the argumentative research essay?

Which kind of term paper will you write?

a. One where all arguments support aim
b. One where the majority of arguments support aim while a minority oppose it
c. One where there is a balance of arguments

Which standard social science outline will you use?

- ❑ Will Appendix C or Appendix D be required?
- ❑ Are you required to create a computer file of Appendix C or D?
- ❑ Did you create your required social science outline?
- ❑ Did you make a backup copy of your completed outline file in a separate storage device?
- ❑ Do you know how to use research priorities to complete your outline?
- ❑ Do you know how to write a coherent term paper based on your completed outline?

Can you visualize your research and writing?

- ❑ Can you follow the diagram plans to do your research and writing?
- ❑ Are you ready to start with priority-one items in the next two chapters?

Recommended Web Sites

An overview of argument from the Dartmouth Writing Program at Dartmouth College: http://www.dartmouth.edu/~writing/materials/faculty/pedagogies/argument. shtml

An overview of writing arguments from Writing Resources at Colorado State University: http://writing.colostate.edu/guides/documents/argueoverview/index.cfm

Recommended Readings

On research and writing:

Muth, F.M. (2006). *Researching and writing: A portable guide*. Boston: Bedford/ St. Martin's.

On visualizing the research and writing process:

Odell, L. & Katz, S.M. (2006). *Writing in a visual age*. Boston: Bedford/St. Martin's.

Robertson, H. (1991). *The research essay*. Ottawa: Piperhill.

Sawers, N. (2002). *Ten steps to help you write better essays & term papers*. (3rd ed.). Edmonton, AB: NS Group.

Chapter 2

Researching to Create an Aim and Arguments

To start you on your research for your term paper, this chapter highlights the first-priority items of the basic social science argumentative format and process. It will show you how to create an aim and arguments. Here is a general list of what will be presented:

1. Start with a topic, subject area, or question.
2. Know how to create an aim.
3. Research to create arguments.
4. Develop your aim from your arguments.

2.1 How Do I Choose a Topic, Subject Area, or Question?

Before you start on a topic, you should know what the word *topic* means. You must also determine if you are to choose your own topic or if your instructor will be choosing the topic for you.

2.1.1 You Must Know the Meaning of *Topic*

When you start your first social science term paper, you will hear the word *topic*. According to Stewart et al. (2004), a topic is a general area of interest that needs to be developed (pp. 162–164). For Corbett and Connors (1999), a topic is a general subject area that you explore in depth (pp. 27–31). In other words, a topic is a general area of interest or subject matter that will be explored or developed into a possible term paper.

There are other words besides the word *topic* that are used to indicate a general interest to be explored, including the following:

- Subject area
- Problem area
- General issue

Here are two examples worded as topics, subject areas, problem areas, or general issues:

- Teen runaways
- Alcohol abuse

Another way to word a topic is as a question. The following table gives examples:

For teen runaways:	*For alcohol abuse:*
• What about teens who run away?	• Who abuses alcohol?
• Where do teens run to?	• When do people abuse alcohol?

For a beginning student, having a general topic (or subject area, problem area, issue, or question) is helpful. It gives you a place to start your research. There are two ways to get a topic: (1) your topic is assigned or (2) you are free to choose your own topic.

2.1.2 You Are Assigned a Topic

An assigned topic means that your instructor may require you to do a research term paper on a certain topic. The reasons for this might be as follows:

- Because the topic is an important part of your course work
- So you can learn a certain part of your course work in more detail

There are at least two noteworthy benefits to you of having an assigned topic:

1. You know that the topic is *part of* and *fits in* with your course.
2. The *words* of your assigned topic are part of your course or field of studies.

Both of these benefits also apply when you are allowed to choose your own topic.

2.1.3 You Choose Your Own Topic

Some reasons an instructor will have for letting you choose your own topic include the following:

- You are more motivated to explore your interests.
- You will learn how your personal interests can be turned into professional ones related to your course work or studies.

If you are allowed to choose your own topic for your term paper, you *must* still fulfill the previous requirements:

- Your topic must be part of and fit in with your course.
- The words of your topic must be part of the course or subject area that you are studying.

Your chosen topic will mean different things to instructors who teach different courses, subjects, or fields of studies called a *discipline* (which refers to a branch of knowledge like anthropology, psychology, or sociology). Various instructors will look at your topic from the point of view of their field of studies. Your topic must fit into their discipline and be worded accordingly. To guide you, here are examples of teen runaways and alcohol abuse and possible wording for different courses:

Course/discipline	Teen runaways	Alcohol abuse
Anthropology	Culture of teen runaways	Alcohol abuse in different cultures
Psychology	Personality traits of teen runaways	Alcohol abuse and perception
Sociology	Social relations of teen runaways	Alcohol abuse and the family
Social services	Shelter for teen runaways	Helping those who abuse alcohol go to detox

Note that the wording for each one of these general examples (teen runaways, alcohol abuse) differs depending on the course. That is, the same example is worded differently to suit each course.

The words used in the topics, so far, are everyday, common words. These words may or may not be used by researchers. Social science researchers may use different words. For example:

- The everyday word *teen* may be substituted by the research word *adolescent*.
- The everyday words *alcohol abuse* might become *chemical dependence*.

You can find different synonyms for your topic by looking in dictionaries and encyclopedias for your field of studies, which we will present later in this chapter.

Instead of coming up with just one topic you should have at least two to three topics. This is in case you have difficulty finding enough research references for your chosen topic. There may be a variety of reasons for not finding as many research references as your instructor requires, such as that the research is written in another language or that the material is not readily available. Hence, you would then move on to your second choice and research it.

Tips

Consider doing a term paper from the standpoint of a participant you are researching. For instance, think about writing a term paper from the standpoint of a runaway teen or the parents of such a teen. As well, you might consider writing a paper from the point of view of a community or social service worker who is helping a runaway teen. Check with your instructor to see if researching and writing this kind of a term paper would be acceptable.

Once you have a number of possible topics for your term paper, you should consult with your instructor about them. This is helpful to you because it means that the words and ideas are much more likely to be part of your course work. Pay particular attention to your instructor's comments about your topic(s) even if they might seem minor to you. These comments are meant to help you with your wording, ideas, and research.

The overall benefit of having a topic(s) is that it helps you get started on your research. However, *a topic is not an aim*. A topic is a good place to start your term paper, but you still have to develop your topic into an aim.

2.2 How Do I Create an Aim?

To create an aim for your term paper, you have to know the meaning of an aim in the social sciences and how to write it in a sentence. Once you understand these basics, you can then go on to create your first aim from your arguments.

2.2.1 You Must Know the Meaning of *Aim*

In the previous chapter the word *aim* was used in a general way to refer to the overall position or stance for your term paper. The word *aim* was used instead of *thesis*, although both have the same general meaning. You should know that there are other similar words that are used in the social sciences, including

- purpose,
- focus, and
- theme.

Each one of these words can readily be substituted for *aim*. The reason these words, including *aim*, are used instead of *thesis* is to emphasize that there are additional requirements in the social sciences to present your overall opinion or focus. A beginning meaning for an *aim* in the social science is this:

- "The use of two differently worded ideas from a field of studies that express a general stance or position supported by convincing arguments."

This section will only clarify what is assumed in understanding an aim; the features related to argument will be presented in the next section. We refer to these assumptions as principles (which means that they are ways, actions, or conditions to follow) in order to create an aim in the social sciences.

There are four principles that you must know and follow to create an aim. These principles are related but will be presented one at a time:

1. There must be two ideas written in words or phrases in your aim.
2. These two ideas must be a part of your course or field of studies.
3. The two ideas must be different.
4. A relationship must be stated between these two different ideas that present an overall position.

Following, we clarify each one of these principles.

1. There Must Be Two Ideas Written in Words or Phrases in Your Aim

An aim in the social sciences must have at least two ideas that are written in words or phrases. This means that one idea will not do:

- The words *teen runaway* are not an aim because there is only one idea.
- The phrase *alcohol abuse* is not an aim because there is only one idea.

Likewise, an attempt to turn one idea into a question for an aim will also not be acceptable.

Example:

Who are teen runaways?

What is alcohol abuse?

These are not acceptable aims because there must be two ideas presented in an aim. Here are examples of two ideas for possible aims:

Teen runaways and homelessness

Teen runaways and deviant behaviour

Alcohol abuse and memory loss

Alcohol abuse and Fetal Alcohol Spectrum Disorder (FASD)

For the above, *teen runaways* is one idea and *deviant behaviour* is another. Likewise, *alcohol abuse* is one idea and *memory loss* is another. There must be at least two ideas in your aim. This book presents only two as a starting point.

2. The Two Ideas Must Be Worded to Be Part of Your Course or Field of Studies

The main reason that the ideas in your aim must be worded in a particular way is that each course or field of studies has its own basic language. The general language for each field of studies consists of concepts. A *concept* is a word or phrase that expresses a mental image or an abstract idea. Your two ideas must be worded in the language of concepts that come from your course, field of studies, or discipline.

Just as the wording of a topic must be a part of a field of studies (see table on p. 37), the same is true for an aim. The ideas, worded as concepts in your aim, are the basic language with which each field of studies communicates. If the words or ideas of your topic do not fit in with your course or field of studies, then you have to reword them to make them relevant. Your instructor may be able to help you by suggesting some concepts to consider in creating an aim relevant to your studies. If it is not possible to reword the aim, find another topic and develop another aim.

3. The Two Ideas or Concepts Must Be Different

Your aim must contain two different ideas or concepts. Notice that the examples from the first principle that presented two ideas were different. That is,

- the idea or concept of teen runaway is *different* from deviant behaviour;
- the concept of alcohol abuse is *different* from memory loss.

Your social science term paper will be about two different ideas or concepts and their relationship.

4. A Relationship Must Be Stated between These Two Different Ideas or Concepts that Presents an Overall Position

The relationship between these two different ideas or concepts will be your overall position, or stand, which you will be presenting in your aim. The wording of the relationship between your two different ideas or concepts will be your central idea, which you want to communicate to your instructor in your term paper.

Examples:

Teen runaways will most likely be socialized into a deviant lifestyle.

Teen runaways tend to come from dysfunctional families.

Abusing alcohol may develop into memory loss.

Alcohol abuse is likely to lead to spousal abuse.

Each of these examples presents something about how you see these two different ideas as related. Your aim must be worded in such a way that you say something about the relationship between these two ideas or concepts. What you say in your aim about that relationship is your overall stance or position for your term paper.

2.2.2. You Must Know How to Create an Aim Sentence

Your first aim should be written as a proper sentence or question. Your sentence or question has to include all four of the preceding principles in order to be considered a proper aim by your instructor. As well, you should include a key word in your aim sentence or present your question in such a way that it indicates clearly to your instructor that this is your aim.

Following are some examples of aim sentences:

The aim of this term paper is to show that teen runaways may be socialized into a deviant lifestyle.

The purpose of this paper is to highlight that alcohol abuse may result in a child with FASD.

Following are examples of aims presented as questions:

The main question addressed in this paper is this: Do teen runaways become street kids?

Does alcohol abuse contribute to spousal abuse? That is the central problem of this term paper.

Note that there are two things that you need to convey to your instructor about your aim sentence or question:

- You must have a properly worded sentence or question. It must be grammatically correct so that your instructor can understand it.
- You have to say that this is your aim sentence or main question. *For a beginning student's term paper, your instructor should have no doubt what your aim is.*

Here are some *problems to avoid* in writing your aim sentence or central question:

- Do not use similar words to *aim* (such as *purpose, focus,* or *theme*) anywhere else in your term paper. Doing this may indicate that you have more than one aim and will make your case confusing to read.
- Do not omit any of the principles of creating an aim. This will weaken the aim for your term paper.
- You must have an aim sentence or main question for a social science research term paper.

| Tips | If you leave out an aim or do not have one, then you do not have a term paper. |

2.2.3 You Must Know How to Create Your Aim from Your Arguments

One way to create an aim for a beginning student is this:

- Start by creating arguments using reference sources from research.
- Then, develop a corresponding aim sentence about your arguments.

This way of creating an aim is called either the bottom-up approach (Norton & Green, 2003, pp. 31–36) or the inductive approach (Kirszner & Mandell, 2004, pp. 539–540). Both terms have a similar meaning. That is, both approaches involve the general process of going from specific arguments to a general aim for your term paper. Particular arguments about a topic are created first, and then an aim is developed about these arguments. The inductive or bottom-up approach is the one used here.

The benefits of starting this way are that

- the aim is based on the kind of arguments that have been created using research reference sources, and
- there are arguments to support the aim that is created.

The wording of your aim will be based on the kind of arguments that you created from researching various reference sources. This avoids the problem of developing an arbitrary aim on a topic and then discovering little information on that topic. Also, your arguments will determine the stance or position of your aim. As a beginning student you will learn that it is your arguments that will determine your view despite any preconceived notions that you might have about your topic.

Reminder

If your instructor has approved your topic of teen runaways, from a participant's standpoint, your aim must also be based on the arguments that you create. That is, the arguments that you create about a participant will determine your aim.

As well, different kinds of arguments on a topic will lead to a different aim. That is why another student working on the same topic as you but with different arguments will have a different aim.

As your arguments change or are altered based on your research, this will subsequently involve changing your aim (view, opinion, or stance). The arguments and aim are thus interrelated. Your aim must have supporting arguments; and your arguments must have a corresponding aim.

As you gain more research and writing experience through additional courses, you might begin with a possible aim and then search for related arguments. This research process is called a top-down approach (Norton & Green, 2003, pp. 36–41) or a deductive approach (Reinking et al., 2007, pp. 154–155). Both approaches have a similar meaning, and both refer to undertaking research as a process that starts from a general aim, which then seeks particular arguments to support it.

This deductive approach is very useful if you already have some familiarity with research and reference sources, especially in a particular area of interest. Essentially, you would have some prior knowledge of research and reference sources to guide you. As a beginning student, you will need to add the deductive approach to that of the inductive one presented here. Knowing both the inductive and deductive approaches is vital for further research.

One idea that both approaches use is that of a *working aim* or *tentative thesis*:

- A working aim (or tentative thesis) means that your stance, position, or view of the ideas being researched is preliminary or tentative.
- A working aim is a guess of what your aim might be, knowing that it will likely be revised or reworded, depending on the arguments that you present.
- For the inductive approach to research, you might refer to your first attempt at wording your aim as a working aim to see how the wording relates to the kind of arguments you have. It may take several tries at a working aim to be able to finalize your aim in relation to your arguments.
- For the deductive approach, a similar process exists. Starting with a working aim on a topic, your arguments will determine the final wording of your aim.

Both approaches use the idea of a working aim to help finalize the wording of an aim based on the actual arguments being presented.

A working aim is helpful because it indicates what your thinking is about the ideas in an aim. As a researcher, you must be open-minded and flexible enough to revise your thinking based on the arguments that you actually have.

2.3 How Do I Research to Create Arguments?

This section presents what is generally meant by an argument and offers suggestions on where you can obtain arguments. Record and keep track of your arguments in the first social science outline, including your reference sources. As your arguments are created, you can then suggest a working aim. After you have made the required number of arguments and have a working aim to go with them, review your work so far with your instructor.

2.3.1 You Must Know the Meaning of *Argument*

In the previous chapter, the word *argument* was used to refer to reasons or points and their supporting evidence to advance an aim. An argument consists of two related parts:

- The point being made
- The evidence to support that point

Both parts are required to make an argument. A single argument, then, consists of one point and the evidence to support that point to convince the reader (your instructor).

The words *point* or *reason* in an argument refer to a sentence that presents at least two or three ideas. That is, a point or reason will usually be a statement or sentence that consists of at least two or three ideas. As a start, the number of ideas in a point is kept small deliberately to make them manageable for a beginning student.

The point of an argument will usually contain the two ideas of the aim sentence plus one further idea. For example, here is an aim sentence:

> The aim of this paper is to show that teen runaways are very likely to be involved in deviant behaviour.

The two main ideas in the aim are *teen runaways* and *deviant behaviour*.
Here is an example of a point in an argument about the aim sentence:

> Teen runaways are highly likely to be involved in the deviant behaviour of stealing.

The additional idea to the aim sentence is the point that is being made about *stealing*. That is, stealing is one kind of deviant behaviour that involves teen runaways. As a point for an argument, there must also be supporting evidence to the point of stealing. Essentially, this added idea of the point in the argument is linked to (or must relate to) the ideas in the aim.

There are a number of things to note about the use of the word *point*, starting with other words that may be used:

- Other words in place of the word *point* that can be used are *reason* or *main point*. It is in this way that you can use the phrase: *The point of this argument is . . .*
- Recall that one argument consists of a point and supporting evidence. As such, one argument consists of one point (or reason or main point) for now. Only one point or reason is required for one argument.
- As well, Norton and Green (2006) highlight that each point must be distinctive from any other point. That is, each point must have a separate meaning and cannot overlap with any other point (p. 55). Each point that you present must be different from the rest.

A point or reason in an argument is different from the evidence supporting it. According to Booth et al. (2008), *evidence* is a statement of a shared and public fact (p. 131). A fact is offered to support the point of your argument and would not be questioned by your instructor (p.131). Evidence is thus *different* from the point that you present.

Your instructor may use other words besides *evidence*. Here is a list of some of these words:

Information	Data (quantitative: numbers; qualitative: descriptions, case studies)	Proof
Statistics	Examples (including perhaps personal experience)	Illustrations

These words suggest the various kinds of evidence, results, or findings, sometimes referred to as facts, that you will need.

> Can you use personal experience as evidence?
> * Some instructors will permit, even encourage, the use of personal experience as an example of a point while others will not.
> * You will have to check with your instructor to see if descriptions of personal experience are within the boundary of acceptable evidence for your course or studies.

Based on this brief meaning of *evidence,* you may wonder how much evidence is enough to make your point convincing. Here are some guidelines about using evidence for your first social science term paper:

* You must have a least one fact for evidence.
* If you do not have any evidence for a point, then you do not have an argument. What you have is an opinion. An entire term paper consisting only of points is not acceptable because it lacks evidence to create arguments.
* If your term paper consists predominantly of descriptions of an event, issue, or people, without making a number of points, then you do not have an acceptable term paper. Here, your term paper would lack points to create arguments.
* Having one or two more facts ensures that you have corroborating evidence to support each point.
* For now, a limit on research evidence would be no more than two or three findings per point.

2.3.2 You Must Look for Quality Research Sources

Before you start your research, whether on-line or in your college library, keep in mind that you are looking for quality sources. One excellent indicator of a quality source is that it has undergone peer review. A *peer review* means that a number of scholars or specialists in the subject area have critically evaluated the work and recommended that it be published. Peer reviews provide a variety of checks on a work, such as accuracy and professional standards. They help to control the quality of what is published. Other sources will be useful to you as well. You may need to verify with other works the information that these sources provide.

Your overall research goal is to look through a variety of sources, most likely books and articles, that you think will be useful to create a working bibliography. The word *bibliography* refers to the list of research sources that you consulted on the topic of your term paper. Searching on-line or in the library to create this list of sources that you *may* use is your working bibliography.

Reminder

A term paper topic written from a participant's standpoint will be more convincing if you have research sources. Find and relate research sources to your participant's ideas and descriptions.

You should search for a variety of sources on your topic whether on-line or in print. Your search will most likely involve sources from related fields of study. Search for quality sources among the following:

Books or E-Books

Books may be in print or available on-line as e-books. Look for reputable, scholarly publishers, such as Oxford, Pearson.

- Check the preface and introduction for the author, the book's purpose, and the research methodology.
- Quality information is also indicated by books with reference sources and a bibliography. Books without these may contain less reliable information.
- Many people write books that may relate to your topic, such as a journalist's investigation of a topic or a politician's autobiography. Use such information appropriately and double-check it as necessary.

Journal and Periodical Articles

There are two general kinds of sources for articles: journal articles and articles in general periodicals. Both are usually available in print and on-line.

- The word *journal* in journal article refers to the professional magazines in which social scientists publish their work and research findings. All fields of study have professional associations that publish academic research articles in their journals. Many are peer reviewed and have high-quality standards. (Ask your instructor for some of the names of journals that might be useful in writing your term paper.)
- Many related fields to the one that you are studying may have useful articles in their journals. You should also consult articles in these related fields.
- An article in a general periodical is meant to be read by the layperson. Articles in general periodicals present information on current topics, questions, and opinions. (Examples are *Psychology Today, The Economist.*)
- You can check the index of topics in the *Readers Guide to Periodical Literature.* You will find this index in the reference section of your library.

Government Publications and Reports

Various levels of government, from local to federal, and their departments produce reports and statistical information.

- There are numerous official publications about laws, policies, issues, and regulations.
- There are government census data (for every 5 or 10 years) although you will have to look elsewhere for more current information.
- You must assess government information (or an organization hired to produce a study for the government) based on the purpose, research methods, and data-collection method.

Newspaper and Magazine Articles

Most well-known magazines (e.g., *Time*, *Newsweek*) and newspapers (e.g., *The New York Times*, *The Globe and Mail*) are on-line and can be consulted for current events. You may use such information to explore a current issue or problem in depth.

Web Sites

Overwhelming material is available on the Internet. Many students simply start their research by typing the keywords of their topic into a search engine to see what happens. Here are some on-line results using the keywords *teen runaways*:

- Google—316 000 results, yielding general information and available help
- Google scholar—13 000 articles, yielding various journals and no sequence of years

Here are some results using the keywords *street kids*:

- Google—about 200 million results
- Google scholar—over 800 000 articles

The information from the preceding two results was interesting but not really useful for a social science term paper. The next section will suggest how to use the Internet for research and how to find better quality information on it.

2.3.3 Where Do I Research to Create Arguments?

While the nature of research has changed and will continue to do so as technology evolves, at present there are two general ways for you to obtain points and evidence for arguments:

- Internet research
- Library research

On the Internet

There are different ways to use the Internet for your research. If your social science topic is unfamiliar, you can use the Internet as a way to learn something about that topic.

You can use the Internet to get a brief overview of an unfamiliar topic. An overview of your topic means to obtain some background information that will help you to understand it. Start with the correct spelling and general meaning of the words of a topic. As well, attempt to determine the importance and extent of some of the major issues or problems of your topic. To get started you can use

- dictionaries and
- encyclopedias.

Dictionaries: You can use a dictionary for the correct spelling of the words in your topic(s) and what your topic means. There are three kinds of dictionaries to note:

1. A general-use dictionary gives you the correct spelling of a word and what it means in everyday use. Examples include the following:

    http://dictionary.reference.com

    http://www.yourdictionary.com

    http://www.alphadictionary.com/index.shtml

    http://www.merriam-webster.com

Reminder

You do not need to reference words that you looked up and used from a general-use dictionary since anyone can look up that definition.

2. A dictionary specific to a field of studies gives you the spelling and meaning of a word used in a specific field of studies. Examples include the following:

    An on-line dictionary of anthropology: http://www.anthrobase.com/Dic/eng/

    An on-line dictionary of psychology: http://allpsych.com/dictionary/

    An on-line dictionary of social sciences (Canadian emphasis): http://bitbucket.icaap.org/dict.pl?alpha=P/

3. A dictionary on specific topics of a field of studies or related fields gives you the spelling and meaning of a word within a specified topic. An example:

    An on-line dictionary of street drug slang: http://www.drugs.indiana.edu/drug-slang.aspx

Encyclopedias: An encyclopedia contains essays that you can use to help you understand your topic. Just like dictionaries, there are three general kinds of encyclopedias (you will most likely have to sign up to use encyclopedias on specific fields and topics):

1. A general-use encyclopedia gives the everyday understanding of topics or problems. Examples include the following:

    http://encarta.msn.com/Default.aspx

    http://en.wikipedia.org/wiki/Main_Page/

Wikipedia—a free on-line general-use encyclopedia	
Do	*Avoid*
use it to get a start on a topic, such as • a general meaning of your topic, • some of the issues involved, or • possible ideas.	using it as a reference source in your term paper because the evidence has not been peer reviewed, so the evidence may not be credible.

2. An encyclopedia for specific fields of study gives the understanding of a topic or problem specific to a field of studies. An example of an encyclopedia of psychology with links to sites:

http://www.psychology.org/links/

An example of an encyclopedia of sociology:

http://www.sociologyencyclopedia.com/public/

3. An encyclopedia on specific topics for a field of studies or related fields gives you the understanding of a topic or problem related to fields of study.
An example of an encyclopedia of women's studies:

http://gem.greenwood.com/wse/wseIntro.jsp

An example of an on-line encyclopedia of drug abuse:

http://www.nlm.nih.gov/medlineplus/ency/article/001945.htm

> If you are unsure about using a dictionary or encyclopedia as an acceptable reference source, ask your instructor before your paper is due or cite it to avoid plagiarism.

Boolean operators: To assist you in finding information, you will need some basic familiarity with Boolean logic to search on-line or in your library. Boolean logic refers to the ways that words can be combined for your search. The most common beginning words are *and*, *or*, and *not*.

Operator	*Meaning*
And or *+ sign*	Link two words using the word *and* or the *+* (*plus*) sign to narrow your search.
Example	Street+children Your search is narrowed to those sources where these words are kept together.
Or or *– sign*	Use *or* or the *–* (*minus*) sign to find sources that contain one or the other word.
Example	Street–children Your search is expanded to sources that contain *street* and sources that contain *children*.
Not	Use *not* to narrow a search.
Example	Street+children not China Your search will contain all street children except those with China.

If you are unfamiliar with Boolean search, the following link to Web tutorials will help you. (It is definitely worthwhile to do a tutorial to grasp the basics of searching.) The link is from California State University at Bakersfield: http://www.csub.edu/tlc/enact/boolean.html

Evaluate the Quality of Your Internet Research Sources

Not all on-line information is of the reliable or valid quality that you will require. You will have to evaluate your research sources to determine the quality of information that is provided. Following are some general guidelines to help you assess Web sites and the information that they provide.

Is it an identifiable and reputable source? Determine if the source hosting the Web site is easily identifiable and reputable. For instance, is the Web site hosted by an identifiable

- scholarly association (e.g., American Sociological Association [ASA], Canadian Sociology and Anthropology Association [CSAA])?
- educational institution (e.g., a college or university)?
- government or government department, at local to federal levels?
- academic publisher (e.g., Oxford, Pearson)? (Note that many scholarly publishers of introductory textbooks have reputable Web sites listed in them.)
- reputable organization (e.g., scientific, business, labour)?

Avoid all other Web sites for your research term paper, such as those with no author, those that are racist or sexist, etc.

Is there peer review of the Web site's information? More reliable information will come from Web sites that indicate that their information is peer reviewed. Check to see if you can determine this easily. Information from sites that are not peer reviewed is also of value. You may need to check with your instructor about these sites.

Is the information current? Check the date of the Web site as well as the dates of the articles to determine if the information is current.

Did you compare information? Compare the information from one Web site with another to see if you can confirm the information. Check to see why the information holds up from these sites or why there is a difference if it does not.

Reminder

Many college and university library Web sites have statements and handouts on evaluating Internet sources for research. Check out your local college or university library Web site to see if it contains additional material to what we provide here. Talk to your instructor if you are unsure about any Web site or reference source before you write your term paper.

How to Read Your Sources to Obtain Arguments

You will need time and effort to read your sources to determine how they will relate to your topic or part of your topic. There are a number of ways to help you determine whether the books, articles, and on-line sources will provide you with the points and evidence that you are looking for to create credible arguments.

Here is a quick summary of how to read your sources to determine if they might be useful to you. (The following information has been adapted from Booth et al., 2008, pp. 76–77.)

Source	Skim or read . . .
Book	• Index (check for keywords and pages on your topic) • First and last paragraphs in chapters with keywords • Introduction and summary chapters • Last chapter, especially first and last two or three pages
Edited book	• Introduction • Chapter titles and first and last page of relevant chapters • Bibliography for more books or articles on your topic
Article	• Abstract, introduction, and conclusion • First and last page of article with no headings • First and last paragraph of sections
On-line source	• Abstract, introduction, overview, summary

For those Web sites where you found relevant material:

• Save the Web sites in your outline.
• Record the URL and date retrieved as necessary for APA style referencing.

In the Library

The books and journal articles by reputable publishers available at your library, in print and on-line, have been screened to ensure that they meet the standards of their respective discipline or profession. This will help you find appropriate social science sources relatively efficiently.

Here are some helpful ways to do your library research:

• Take tours or services offered by your library to learn where different materials are kept (e.g., books, general periodicals, government documents, reference materials) and how to use them.
• Ask librarians to assist you in finding information (e.g., reference desk, help desk, on-line assistance).
• Search your library on-line for various sources, including books and articles on your topic.
• Use the library's on-line catalogue (it contains a list of all of the library's holdings). Use the keywords of your topic to search for materials. Try various keywords (e.g., *teen runaways, runaway teens, street kids, homeless youth*).
• If your search is unsuccessful on your chosen topic, ask for assistance. Librarians are familiar with key search words as well as the location of material and sources to help you. Many college and university libraries have on-line help.
• Check interlibrary loan since not all libraries carry the same books. Ask how long it will take to get a book from another library.
• Use electronic databases (these contain millions of journal articles provided

by on-line services like EBSCO or ProQuest). Start with a general term, then narrow your search to your specific topic. You will get a list of abstracts or summaries of articles and reference source information. More full-length articles will be provided that you can save or e-mail to yourself.

Record and save all relevant information in your outline. If you are unsure about keeping material (e.g., an abstract), create a separate research file (and possibly a research folder) for your topic and save it there.

2.3.4 Record Your Arguments and References in Your Outline

In addition to your standardized social science outline, there are other ways to record your arguments. These include the following:

- File cards or index cards are handy for recording information when reading a book or article. It is easy to reorganize arguments and evidence to suit your purpose.
- A laptop computer or other digital device is convenient to record points and evidence. You may be tempted, however, to record too much information.

Reminder

If you have recorded points, evidence, and references on index cards, on paper, or to a digital device, remember to transfer this information to your outline.

This book recommends two general steps to help you create arguments and record their references in your outline:

- Create a draft of your arguments in the outline.
- Revise your draft arguments in the outline.

Create Draft Arguments in Outline

Consider the start of creating arguments in your outline as a rough draft. Recall that your overall goal is to create one or two arguments more than what you need, along with reference sources. Here are some suggestions to help you do this:

- Decide if a book or journal article is relevant to your topic and interest. If in doubt, hang on to it or save it.
- Record all your references as a working bibliography in your outline (add the library call number for those materials that have them in case you have to return them and take them out again).
- Make sure that the total number of reference sources in your working bibliography is more than the required minimum.
- If you are unable to get the minimum number of reference sources for your first topic (for whatever reason), then go to your second topic and repeat the previous process.
- If you find too many reference sources, narrow your topic.

How to limit your topic:
- Look for material on only one side (or one part) of your topic, problem, or issue.
- Look for material on either the positive (pro) *or* negative (con) part.

Record your points, evidence, and their sources in the following ways (from Muth, 2006, pp. 107–112):

	Quote	*Paraphrase*	*Summarize*
Meaning	Copy exact words	Restate something in your words	Shorter version, presenting only main points
Reason	Support your point or evidence in words of original	Present information in your words, using fewer words	Much shorter than original
Do not . . .	quote long passages, or copy and paste	follow sentence or pattern of original	summarize unfairly

Do not worry about the sequence of your points and evidence for now. Concentrate on creating arguments. If you have too many arguments, then limit yourself to only one kind.

If you have too many arguments (i.e., 10–12 for a 5-argument paper):
- Look for patterns in your arguments.
- Break your arguments into general groups.
- Do your paper on only one part or group of your arguments.

Here is an example of too many arguments (for a five-argument term paper) on runaway teens, consisting of eleven arguments that have been grouped into two—the reasons to be street kids and what happens to them on the street:

Reasons for becoming street kids	*What happens to runaway teens living on the street*
• Conflict with parents	• Stealing
• Emotional abuse	• Panhandling
• Neglect	• Dealing drugs
• Physical abuse	• Doing drugs
• Sexual abuse	• Violence
	• Prostitution

Suggestions:

- Use the arguments from *either* the reasons for running away or from what happens to runaway teens living on the street.
- Note that *now you are only dealing with one part of your topic.* You may decide to do the other part (or different parts) of this topic for a future term paper.
- *The change in arguments has led to a change in emphasis of the term paper. The focus is now on street kids rather than on teen runaways.*

Here is an example of draft arguments. The arguments have been condensed to save space (references omitted).

1. Point: no point
   Evidence: info on runaway population
2. Point: stealing, theft
   Evidence: percentage data
3. Point: dealing drugs
   Evidence: percentage of kids involved
4. Point: prostitution, obligatory sex
   Evidence: percentage data
5. Point: substance abuse
   Evidence: percentage data
6. Point: panhandling, begging
   Evidence: difference in boys/girls
7. Point: victims of crime
   Evidence: percent assaulted
8. Point: violence among street kids
   Evidence: examples of weapons

- Save your draft argument outline file.
- For now, do not worry if some "arguments" only have a point but no evidence, or evidence and no point.

Revise Draft Arguments in Outline

Before you start to revise your draft argument outline, here is what you should do:

- Make a copy of your original draft argument outline.
- Save it as a separate file.
- Give it a new file name (e.g., "Revised outline v1"—you may want to keep earlier versions and make new versions as you revise).

Check the following in revising your draft argument outline:

- Make sure that one argument consists of a point and related evidence.
- Check to determine if a point is a point (reason, idea) and that your evidence is actually evidence (information, data, or example, not a continuation of your point).
- For points and evidence that cannot be made into arguments, decide if they can be used in your introduction.
- Check that each point and related evidence is a separate argument.
- Word any subordinate or related points and evidence as a separate argument.
- Check reference sources (within points and evidence as well as References section) to make sure that they are complete according to APA standards (see next chapter).
- Formatting of references section of your outline is not necessary for now.

Example of revising draft arguments (condensed to save space):

Draft arguments	Revised arguments
1. Point: no point Evidence: info on runaway population	Use in introduction
2. Point: stealing, theft Evidence: percentage data	1. Keep
3. Point: dealing drugs Evidence: percentage of kids involved	2. Keep
4. Point: prostitution, obligatory sex Evidence: percentage data	Keep 3. Prostitution 4. Obligatory sex
5. Point: substance abuse Evidence: percentage data	5. Keep
6. Point: panhandling, begging Evidence: difference in boys/girls	Use in introduction
7. Point: victims of crime Evidence: percent assaulted	6. Keep
8. Point: violence among street kids Evidence: examples of weapons	Use in introduction

Your goal is to create good, solid arguments that fulfill the requirements for your social science term paper. Revising the draft arguments has reduced the number from a possible eight arguments to six for a five-argument term paper. Having one or two arguments beyond what is required is helpful in case you need to change or drop one as you create your aim.

Once you have settled on your arguments, then proceed to work on your aim.

2.4 How Do I Develop My Aim from My Arguments?

Now you should have a number of arguments that you can use to develop an aim. You will be using inductive reasoning to create your aim because you will be using specific arguments to create a general aim.

2.4.1 First, Create a Working Aim from Your Arguments

Recall that an aim in the social sciences must satisfy a number of conditions. One condition is that there must be at least two concepts. So far, only one concept for the aim has been decided on, and that is the phrase "street kids".

Because there is only one concept here, another concept and a view about these two concepts are still required to create a working aim. There are two steps that may help in creating a working aim:

- Start by wording your potential aim in everyday language.
- Translate the everyday wording of your working aim into the professional language and concepts of your course, discipline, or field of studies.

Use Everyday Wording for Your Working Aim

To create a working aim, begin by looking at what seems to be common to most of your arguments. Recall that you may have narrowed your arguments by grouping them. Use this to help you begin to word your aim.

Examples of possible everyday wording for working aims based on negative arguments of runaway teens living on streets or simply, street kids:

- Street kids are involved in negative behaviours.
- Street kids get caught up in very serious problems.
- Street kids get caught up in negative activities to survive.

With this beginning, you should then word your aim more in the language of a social science. This will mean using an appropriate concept(s) from your course or field of studies.

Then Use Professional Wording for Your Working Aim

There are a number of possibilities here for changing the everyday wording of a working aim into the professional language of your discipline or field of studies. For example:

- Street kids develop their own culture.
- Street kids have to learn negative behaviours in order to survive.
- Street kids get involved in deviant behaviour.

What you are doing here is expressing everyday language in professional terms (and in turn stating what professional wording means in everyday language).

Also, you have to *judge* how well your aim expresses your arguments. In other words, the wording of your aim must be able to include all of your arguments. Note that it may take several attempts at wording before you decide on one working aim.

You must make a *decision* to select one working aim, for now. There may be further modifications to the wording of your working aim, but you need to decide which one to use. Here is an example of the *working aim* that was decided on:

> The aim of this paper is to show that street kids are very likely to be involved in deviant behaviour.

This is a working aim because there are two different concepts (*street kids* and *deviant behaviour*) that are part of the social sciences and because a relationship between the two is expressed. This relationship is expressed in the choice of concepts (*negative behaviour* now is *deviant behaviour*) and the wording between them (i.e., that street kids are *very likely to be involved in* deviant behaviour).

Following is an example of creating an aim from points in arguments.

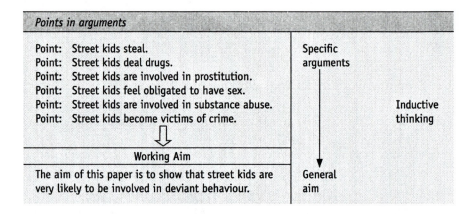

2.4.2 Word Your Arguments to Include Your Aim

Once you have a working aim, work on the actual wording of the points of your arguments in your outline. Word each point to include the two main ideas of your working aim and write this point in a sentence. The wording of your points in proper sentences is important because these sentences will be the first sentence of your paragraph for the point that you are making in one argument.

For example, here is some preliminary wording of points in sentences about street kids and deviant behaviour:

1. Street kids are involved in the deviant behaviour of stealing.

2. Street kids are involved in the deviant behaviour of dealing drugs.

3. Street kids are involved in the deviant behaviour of prostitution.

4. Street kids are involved in the deviant behaviour of obligatory sex.

5. Street kids are involved in the deviant behaviour of substance abuse.

6. Street kids are involved in the deviant behaviour of victims of crime.

This first effort is clearly repetitive and will need to be improved upon. However, this repetition does start the process of putting together the ideas of the working aim with those of the points. From this beginning, these sentences will have to be reworded to show variety and interest in the different points. In revising these sentences, you will have to do the following:

- Judge how well your points relate to your aim.
- Determine if each sentence makes sense. For example, is being a victim of crime really deviant behaviour?
- Decide which sentences make the best case for the concepts that you are using.

Here are examples of revising the wording of the previous sentences:

1. Once you are a street kid you are very likely to become involved in the deviant behaviour of stealing

2. Dealing in drugs is a deviant activity of street kids.

3. Street kids become involved in the deviant behaviour of prostitution.

4. Another form of deviant behaviour related to prostitution is that street kids engage in obligatory sex.

5. One kind of deviant behaviour of street kids is their involvement in substance abuse.

6. Living on the street means that in all likelihood street kids will be victims of a crime. *(Does not really fit with aim, use in introduction?)*

Your revised sentences of points for arguments have to include your aim and make sense. If you are unsure about any points, keep them for now (e.g., point sentence number 6) until you finalize your arguments.

Now, consult with your instructor about the aim, arguments, and references that you have in your outline.

2.4.3 Consult with Your Instructor

So far you have a working aim, related arguments, and reference sources. Here are some things that you need to find out from your instructor:

- Does each argument relate to the aim?
- Are the ideas of the aim included in the arguments?
- Can the aim and arguments be reworded with a concept that will improve them?
- Are there other possible sources to research?

Getting feedback from your instructor is very important. Instructors have different ways of providing feedback, according to the number of students in a class and the kind of class (such as correspondence or on-line courses). An instructor with smaller classes may be able to provide individual consultation, but an instructor with larger classes may not be able to do this. What is important for you is to get some feedback and comments on what you have done so far.

If you are able to see your instructor one-on-one, bring your outline and be prepared to write notes and suggestions as conveyed by your instructor. For other instructors (e.g., on-line), you might submit your social science outline to your instructor and ask for comments and suggestions. Remember to keep a copy of anything submitted to an instructor in case she or he loses it.

In addition, do not hesitate to follow up on any of your instructor's comments or suggestions that you do not understand. Make revisions based on your instructor's comments before proceeding to other parts of the outline.

2.4.4 Revise Your Aim and Arguments

Complete the revisions from your instructor and finalize your aim and arguments. Making revisions to the aim and arguments now is simply *more efficient* than completing everything else for the outline and then having to do those parts over again. Making revisions now will save you a lot of time! If necessary, do the following:

- Research the references that your instructor recommended.
- Reword your aim and arguments as necessary.
- Make a final decision on which specific arguments to keep.

Your decisions should be based on keeping those arguments that

- match the clearest or are the best fit with your aim, and
- have the best evidence.

Once you have revised and completed these first priorities (the aim, arguments, and references), you should then define the concepts in your aim, determine the order of the arguments, and prepare to draft the conclusion.

Chapter Summary

Start with a topic, subject area, or question:

- Know the meaning of *topic*—a subject area to be developed into a term paper.
- Be assigned a topic—worded as part of course.
- Choose own topic—must be worded to fit in with course or field of studies.

Know how to create an aim:

- Know the meaning of *aim*—a stance on two different ideas supported by convincing arguments.
- Follow the four principles to create an aim—there must be two ideas, they must be part of your field of studies, the ideas must be different, and a relationship between them must be stated.
- Know how to create an aim sentence by adding that this is the aim sentence or main question for your term paper.
- Know how to create your aim from your arguments.
- Start by creating arguments from reference sources.
- Develop corresponding aim sentence or working aim from arguments.

Know how to research to create arguments:

- Keep track of aim, arguments, and references by recording them in your outline.
- *Argument* means point and evidence to support that point.
- *Point* refers to idea or reason, and *evidence* means fact or results to support point.
- Look for quality research sources, peer reviewed, to create your working bibliography.

Use other information sources appropriately:

- Research to create arguments can be undertaken on the Internet or in your library.
- For Internet research, start with an overview for an unfamiliar topic.
- Learn basic Boolean operators to help you search.
- Know how to evaluate the quality of your Internet research sources by checking the reputation of the Web site, determining whether the information is peer reviewed and current, and comparing information to substantiate it.
- Learn to read your sources efficiently to find information for arguments.
- For library research, search for arguments in relevant sources on your topic. If necessary, ask for assistance in searching and obtaining information.
- Record your arguments and references in your outline.
- In addition to your outline, use other ways to start recording arguments, including file cards, laptop, other digital devices.

- Create a draft of your arguments in the outline by quoting, paraphrasing, and summarizing material from your reference sources.
- If you don't have enough material, go to your second topic; if you have too much material, limit the arguments to one part or group of topic.
- Save draft of arguments in outline; revise to create clear, separate arguments.
- Decide if unused portions of arguments can be used in introduction.
- Make sure you have enough arguments for your term paper as required (plus one or two more).

Develop your aim from your arguments:

- Start creating a working aim from your arguments by what is common to them and wording your aim in everyday language.
- Translate the everyday wording of your aim into the professional language of your field of studies or discipline.
- The wording of your working aim must fulfill the previous four principles required in the social sciences in order to be an acceptable aim.
- Word the points (in your arguments) in a sentence to include the ideas in your aim; record these in your outline.
- Ensure variety in each sentence and that each sentence makes sense; keep uncertain arguments for now.
- Consult with your instructor about each item in your outline—aim, arguments, and reference sources.
- Revise items as directed by your instructor and finalize working aim and arguments.

 ## Checklist for Term Paper Research

Do you have a topic, subject area, or question?
- ❑ Do you have two to three topics that fit into your course or field of studies?

Do you know how to create an aim?
- ❑ Do you know how to create an aim and an aim sentence?
- ❑ Do you know how to create a working aim from your arguments?

Did you research to create arguments?
- ❑ Do you know the meaning of *argument*, *point*, and *evidence*?
- ❑ Do you know how to evaluate the quality of your research sources?
- ❑ Did you start your research with an overview on the Internet?
- ❑ Can you use basic Boolean operators to search for sources?
- ❑ Can you read your sources efficiently to find information for arguments?

❑ Did you check for sources in your library? Did you ask for assistance, on-line or in person, to find research sources for arguments?

❑ Are you recording all relevant materials in your outline (creating a separate file and folder for related research material)?

❑ Do you have enough reference sources and material? If not, go to second topic and repeat process.

❑ If you have too much material, can you limit yourself to part of or one group of arguments of your topic?

❑ Did you save your draft argument outline and make a copy for your revision?

❑ Did you revise draft of arguments to ensure each argument consists of a separate point and has at least one (no more than three) facts of evidence?

❑ Can unused portions of arguments be used in introduction?

❑ Do you have enough required arguments (plus one or two more)?

Did you develop your aim from your arguments?

❑ Did you develop a working aim from what is common to your arguments and state it in everyday language?

❑ Did you translate the everyday wording of your working aim into the professional language of your field of studies or discipline?

❑ Does your working aim fulfill the social science principles of an aim as required?

❑ Did you word each point to include the working aim, and did you write this point in a sentence?

❑ Does the point for each sentence show variety and make sense?

❑ Did you consult with your instructor? What comments did your instructor make about each item in your outline (working aim, arguments, and reference sources)?

❑ Did you revise each item as directed by your instructor?

❑ Did you decide on your final aim and arguments?

Recommended Web Sites

Cannell Library of Clark College in Vancouver, WA—free tutorials and a useful information and research instruction suite (IRIS), including research, deciding on a topic, and research notes:

http://www.clark.edu/Library/iris/index.shtml

Dartmouth Writing Program—useful information on researching your topic, including working with sources:

http://www.dartmouth.edu/~writing/materials/student/ac_paper/research. shtml#cite/

Dartmouth Writing Program of Dartmouth College—some materials for students about topic, research, and argument:
http://www.dartmouth.edu/~writing/materials/student/toc.shtml

Effective Writing Program, University of Calgary—see the various resources for writing in different disciplines:
http://efwr.ucalgary.ca/writinginthedisciplines/

Intute (UK)—a free on-line Web resource for information in the social sciences:
http://www.intute.ac.uk/socialsciences/

San Diego State University—links to hot topics:
http://infodome.sdsu.edu/research/guides/hot/supersites.shtml

Tidewater Community College (US)—research paper and argument topic ideas:
http://www.tcc.edu/students/resources/writcent/HANDOUTS/writing/restopics.htm

University of Colorado at Boulder—social science research resources:
http://polsci.colorado.edu/RES/research.html

Recommended Readings

Deciding on a topic and reference sources:
Roe, S.C., & den Ouden, P.H. (Eds.). (2003). *Designs for disciplines: An introduction to academic writing.* Toronto: Canadian Scholars' Press.

Chapter 3

Referencing Your Sources: Some Basic APA Styles

This chapter presents some of the common APA styles that many social science instructors require students to use in order to reference or document research resources. Some benefits of using a common APA referencing style for research sources include the following:

- The author and year are at the beginning of the reference. You can judge quickly how recent and relevant the source is that you are using.
- A common style makes tracing ideas, sources, and original work easy. You do not have to rely on or trust someone else's interpretation or version of another work. As well, your instructor can easily check your sources.

Students new to the *Publication Manual* (2010) of the APA can consult the Web site http://www.apastyle.org for a free tutorial on some of the basic APA styles; click on the *Learning APA Styles* tab. As well, the Web site provides more detailed referencing information and will be able to present more current style changes than the *Publication Manual*.

The beginning referencing styles presented here consist of two general parts. These are

1. in-text citations and
2. references.

A sample references page is provided at the end of this chapter.

3.1 How Do I Use In-Text Citations?

3.1.1 First, Know the Meaning of *Citation*

In-text citations are references to sources that are presented in the text of your term paper or book review (as well as an article critique). When you write the name of an author(s) or a report from which information has been used in your term paper or book review, that is *citing* or a *citation*. The citation indicates the source of your quotation, information, or idea. Citations or references in your term paper or book review are necessary. Most instructors prefer that you use a lot of citations to indicate some familiarity with the research sources of your aim and topic.

3.1.2 Know When to Use In-Text Citations

You *must* use in-text citations to give credit for an idea, point, example, direct quote, or anything from someone else. Otherwise, you are committing plagiarism.

There are, however, instances when no citation is required. For example, no citations are required for common knowledge. *Common knowledge* refers to ideas or information that are available or known generally to anyone. For instance, a definition from a general-use dictionary does not need to be cited because anyone can look up the meaning of that word. Similarly, you would not need to cite that Freud was a major figure in psychology because that is a well-known fact. On the other hand, when you use a definition from an author in your field of studies, you must cite that author because you are using that particular author's meaning for your purpose. As well, when you refer to specific ideas or information from Freud's theory of personality, you must cite that. If you are unsure about citing an idea or information, check with your instructor or provide a citation.

You will use in-text citations throughout your term paper or book review. For example, you will use them in your definitions, throughout your arguments, or wherever you have used someone else's point or evidence. By citing research and writing sources, you learn how much work has been done before and how useful that work is to your aim or purpose.

3.1.3 Know How to Format In-Text Citations

To get started with in-text citations, here is a general format for including reference sources in the text of a term paper or book review. In the example below the format is in parentheses:

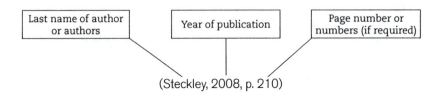

Include a page number when you are quoting or paraphrasing.

For One Author of a Work (Book, Article, Audiovisual Material)

Use the last name of the author and the year of the book or article. For audiovisual material, use the last name of the producer and director and year. There are two ways to do this:

- If you mention the author's last name in your sentence, place the year in parentheses right after the name:

  Letts (2008) argues that . . .

- If you do not mention the author's name in the sentence, place her or his last name and year at the end of the sentence:

Much sociological research comes from people's real-life experiences (Brym, 2004).

For a Quotation

When you quote an author, you must provide the page number(s). The page number comes after the year or at the end of the quote:

- For one page, the abbreviation "p." is used:

Ritzer (2006) argues that "the principles of the fast-food industry are coming to dominate more and more sectors of American society as well as of the rest of the world" (p. 5).

- For two or more pages, the abbreviation "pp." is used:

"Rules and procedures cover everything, eliminating decision making for workers" (Royle, 2006, pp. 179–180).

A short quote has fewer than 40 words and is included in the text of your term paper. Quotation marks start and end the quote. It looks like this:

"The military has been pressed to offer fast food on both bases and ships" (Ritzer, 2006, p. 12).

A long quotation is 40 or more words in length and is treated as a separate block of text. Every line of the text is indented the same, i.e., five spaces or one-half inch. The quotation is double-spaced, and there are no quotation marks for this quote. Do not indent the first line for one paragraph. If your quote is more than two paragraphs, indent the first line of the second paragraph (and other paragraphs) five spaces or one-half inch.

Example of a long quote:

Michael Veseth (2006) has the following perspective on bureaucracy and health care:

A successful visit to a modern health maintenance organization clinic illustrates a bureaucracy at work. The division of labor, both within offices and among specialities, is obvious. The steps of making appointments, gathering information, making diagnoses, planning treatment, performing tests, filling prescriptions, etc., are all discrete and handled by specialists. Information technology is used to share information and coordinate the stages. (p. 352)

For a Quote within a Quote

Use single quotation marks for a short quote within the text and double quotation marks within a longer quote. Note the single quotation marks *within* the following quote.

Example of a quote within a quote:

Veseth (2006) argues that "McDonald's is an excellent example of the process that the great German sociologist Max Weber (1864–1920) called 'formal rationalization'" (p. 352).

A longer block of text is 40 words or more in total and is indented the same as the previous long quote. In the following example, note that the phrase "resurrection of subjugated knowledges" has double quotation marks around it because this is a quote within a long block quotation. Do not use quotation marks around a long quote. Example of a quote within a long quote:

> Pieterse (2006) makes the following argument about hybridization in a postmodern culture:
>
>> If modernity stands for an ethos of order and neat separation by tight boundaries, hybridization reflects a postmodern sensibility of cut 'n' mix, transgression, subversion. It represents, in Foucault's terms, a "resurrection of subjugated knowledges" because it foregrounds those effects and experiences which modern cosmologies, whether rationalist or romantic, would not. (p. 280)

For Summarizing and Paraphrasing

Whenever you summarize or paraphrase another author within the text, you must cite the source, stating author and year. Follow the same referencing style as you would for a quote.

Two Authors:

For two authors of a work, mention both names when you cite them:

- For authors used in a sentence (note the use of the word *and*):

  Parkinson and Drislane (2003) suggest that . . .

- For authors not mentioned in the sentence (note the use of the & symbol):

  This argument has been made before (Parkinson & Drislane, 2003).

Three, Four, or Five Authors:

For three to five authors, mention all the authors the first time that you cite them. After that, use the last name of the first author, with the Latin abbreviation et al. (meaning "and others") following:

- For the first time:

  Smith, Jones, and Lee (2008).

- After that:

  Smith et al. (2008).

Six or More Authors:

For six or more authors, cite the last name of the first author followed by et al. the first time that the in-text citation is presented:

  (Gayle et al., 2009)

An Author Cited by Another Author:

Here an author is cited or quoted by another author in a book or journal article. In the APA style guide, this is referred to as an indirect source. Cite the original author in the text of your term paper and state where you found the information at the end of the citation:

> Lenzer (1975) stated that history is important because it allows us "to attain a critical dimension of self-reflection" (cited in Bailey & Gayle, 2003, p. viii).

A Reprinted Article:
Cite the author or the title of the article followed by the year it was originally published, a forward slash, and the year reprinted:

> (Manifesto of the Chinese People's Liberation Army, 1947/1988)

A Group as Author:
Cite the name the first time it is mentioned, then abbreviate after that. If there is no abbreviation for the group, continue to write out the reference in full:

- For an association for first reference in text:

> (Canadian Mental Health Association [CMHA], 2004)

- For subsequent references for association in text:

> (CMHA, 2004)

A Newspaper Article:
To refer to a newspaper article with no author, present a short title:

> ("Women and Poverty," 2004)

No Author:
If there is no author, use the first few words of the title of the book, article, or reference:

- When no author is given for an article or chapter, use quotation marks:

> . . . on free care ("Investigation continues," 2004)

- When no author is given for the title of a brochure, periodical, or book, italicize:

> . . . the book, *Working with the Media* (2004)

No Year:
If no year is provided in a reference, use the abbreviation n.d. for "no date":

> . . . the argument by Jones (n.d.)

Public Presentation or Lecture:
State the last name of the author and the year in the text, just as you would for an author of a work. Give the complete information in the references section.

Personal Communication:
(*Note:* Do *not* include these in your references page.) Personal communication includes personal interviews, memos, letters, and some electronic communications, such as e-mail or electronic bulletin boards. Cite them only in the text of your term paper or book review.

> J. Smith (personal communication, September 15, 2009)

> (Jones, personal communication, November 15, 2009)

3.1.4 Know How to Refer to Electronic or On-line Sources

On-line reference sources use the same in-text citation format as any other reference source. One main difference for on-line sources, however, concerns page numbers:

- For an electronic source in a portable document format (PDF) with page numbers, give the page number in parentheses:

  (Smith, 2008, p. 4)

- For an electronic source with *numbered paragraphs*, use the abbreviation *para.* or ¶ followed by the number:

  (Smith, 2008, para. 8) *or* (Smith, 2008, ¶ 8)

- For an electronic source with *no numbering*, use the heading and the paragraph number under that heading:

  (Jones, 2008, Organization, para. 15)

For a Government Document

Indicate that your information comes from a Web site. Specify the government or department, and the year:

The Web site *Human Resources and Skills Development* (2004) provides Canadians with the tools to succeed in their workplace and community.

For a Web site

Refer to the author and year of the Web site:

The goals of an introductory sociology class are stated on Brym's (2004) Web site.

Since your in-text citations present an incomplete part of your referencing, you must present the full text of your research sources in the references page.

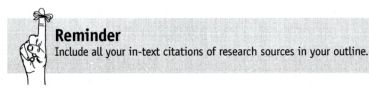

Reminder
Include all your in-text citations of research sources in your outline.

3.2 How Do I Use References?

3.2.1 First, Know the Meaning of *References*

The word *references* generally means "to attribute the sources of your research". In APA style, the references page refers to the list of the full text of all your research sources. For your term paper or book review, you must provide a complete and accurate list of your in-text citations in the required APA style.

3.2.2 Know What to Include in Your References Page

Include in your list only those books, articles, and materials that you *actually used*, which means that they are cited in the text of your term paper or book review (or article critique).

Reminder

Do not include any material that you read and did not cite. Do not include personal communication.

3.2.3 Use the Proper Format for the References Page

Here is a list of general formatting requirements for your references page:

- Place your references list at the end of your term paper.
- On a separate page, type the word *References* (not *Bibliography*) at the top of the page and centre it.
- Start with the last name of the author to create an alphabetical list. Where there is no author, use the article or book title. (*Do not number your references.*)
- After the last name of the author, use initials for first name(s) of author(s).
- Double-space your list.
- Start the first line of each reference on the left-hand margin, and indent all succeeding lines five spaces, or one-half inch.
- Pay particular attention to capitalization, punctuation, use of italics, and so on in the examples.

Reminder

See the sample references page at the end of this chapter for an example of how a references page should look.

Next, we will present some basic formatting for the following:

- Books
- Articles in journals or other periodicals
- Electronic sources
- Audiovisual media

For a Book

The format for referencing a book is as follows:

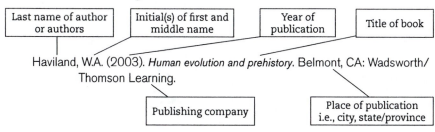

- Start a book reference with the last name of the author followed by the initials of her or his first and middle names.
- Then, give the year the book was published in parentheses followed by a period.
- The title of the book, italicized, comes next. Capitalize only the first word in the title and subtitle, except for all proper nouns (for example, *Toronto, New York, London*), and end with a period.
- If the book is a second or following edition, add the edition in parentheses (e.g., 5th ed.).
- The city and state or province of publication comes next (if there are multiple cities, choose the first one), followed by the name of the publishing company without the words *Publishing, Company*, or *Inc.*

Following are examples:

One Author:

> Bell, M. (2009). *An invitation to environmental sociology.* Thousand Oaks, CA: Pine Forge.

Two Authors:

> Macionis, J.J., & Gerber, L.M. (2004). *Sociology.* (5th ed.) Toronto: Prentice Hall.

Three to Five Authors:

> Henslin, J.M., Glenday, D., Duffy, A., & Pupo, N. (2004). *Sociology: A down to earth approach.* (3rd ed.) Toronto: Pearson.

Six or More Authors:

Give only the last name and initials of the first author, followed by the abbreviation et al.

No Author:

When there is no author, use the title of the book, article, or report. Titles of books are italicized. Do not italicize or put quotes around titles of articles.

Use the title to fit the work within the alphabetized system of the references page. (See sample references page at end of this chapter.)

A Group or Corporation as Author:

Use the name of the organization or group:

> Nishga Tribal Council. (1993). *Nisga'a: People of the Nass River.* Vancouver: Douglas & MacIntyre.

When the author and publisher are the same, type the word *Author* where the name of the publisher would be:

> Canadian Sociology and Anthropology Association. (2003). *Statement of professional ethics.* Montreal: Author.

An Article or Chapter in an Edited Book:

> Connidis, I.A. (2001). Aging. In J.J. Teevan, & W.E. Hewitt (Eds.). *Introduction to sociology.* (7th ed.). (pp. 228–252). Toronto: Prentice Hall.

A Work in a Collection or Textbook:

Always give the primary reference:

> Brym, R.J. (2004). *Society in question: Sociological readings for the 21st century.* (4th ed.). Toronto: Nelson.

All other works included in Brym are presented as follows:

> Charon, J. (1998). Is sociology important? The need for a critical understanding of society. In Brym, pp. 10–15.
>
> Brym, R.J., & Saint-Pierre, C. (1997). Sociology in Canada. In Brym, pp. 16–21.
>
> Tannen, D. (1990). The glass ceiling. In Brym, pp. 28–41.
>
> Schlosser, E. (2001). Kids as customers. In Brym, pp. 42–47.

A Reprinted Article in a Book:

> Manifesto of the Chinese People's Liberation Army. (1988). In P. Cormack (Ed.) *Manifestos and declarations of the twentieth century.* (pp. 23–30). Toronto: Garamond. Reprinted from the *Manifesto of the Chinese People's Liberation Army, 1947.*

3.2.4 Use the Proper Format for Articles in Journals or Other Periodicals

The general pattern for the *full referencing* of articles is as follows:

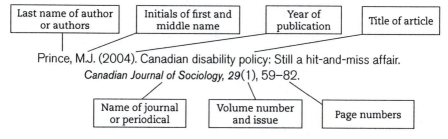

Be aware that no "pp." is used before page numbers for an article (see below).

For a Journal

One Author:

> Mobley, C. (2007). Breaking ground: Engaging undergraduates in social change through service learning. *Teaching Sociology, 35*(2), 125–137.

Two to Six Authors:

> Tsuzi, L.J.S., & Ho, E. (2002). Traditional environmental knowledge and western science: In search of common ground. *The Canadian Journal of Native Studies, 22*(2), 327–360.

Seven or More Authors:

List the first six authors and then use et al.

For a Magazine Article

Snider, M., & Borel, K. (2004, May 24). Stalked by a cyberbully. *Maclean's*, 117, 76–77.

For a Newspaper Article

The Nature Conservancy of Canada. (2004, May 28). Saving Canada's natural masterpieces. *The Globe and Mail*, pp. E1–E3.

For a Book Review in a Journal

Cosgrave, J. (2004). The age of chance: Gambling and western culture [Review of the book *The Age of Chance: Gambling and Western Culture*]. *Canadian Journal of Sociology: Book Reviews, 29*(1), 155–158.

For a Public Presentation or Lecture

Smith, A.B. (2009, October 15). *How can we help the parents of runaway street kids?* Institute for Social Planning. Vancouver: UBC.

For a Video Recording

Miller, C. (Producer). (2002). Critical listening [Video recording]. [Available from the B.C. Learning Connection, Vancouver, B.C.].

For a Report

Canada Mortgage and Housing Corporation & Inuit Tapirisat of Canada. (2001). *Research and consultation project concerning Inuit housing across Canada: Final report/Inuit Tapirisat of Canada.* Ottawa: Canada Mortgage and Housing Corporation.

3.2.5 Use the Proper Format for Electronic Sources

Electronic sources follow the same referencing format as do print sources. Additional elements are added to electronic sources in order to find them. Here are some general referencing and formatting guidelines:

- Use a digital object identifier (DOI) for an on-line source when there is one.
- The DOI may be hidden under a label, like *Article*. It is best to copy and paste the DOI.
- If there is no DOI, use the URL or the homepage URL if there is a subscription.
- For URLs, there is no dot after an Internet address.
- To break up a URL at the end of a line, break it before punctuation. Do not add a hyphen to break the URL.
- The retrieval date is added to the reference when the content is likely to change or be updated.
- A retrieval date is not required when the content is *not* changed or updated.

For an Article from an On-line Journal

Articles with DOIs:

> Mitchell, M.M., Severtson, S.G, & Latimer, W.W. (2008, July). Pregnancy
> and race/ethnicity as predictors of motivation for drug treatment.
> *The American Journal of Drug and Alcohol Abuse, 34*(4), 397–404.
> doi: 10.1080/00952990802082172

Articles without DOIs:

> Atkins, P.J. (2003). Mother's milk and infant death in Britain, circa 1900–1940.
> *Anthropology of Food.* Retrieved from http://www.aofood.org
> /JournalIssues/02/atkins.pdf

For an Article Printed in a Journal and Reproduced On-line

> Irwin, K. (2004). The violence of adolescent life: Experiencing and managing
> everyday threats. [Electronic version]. *Youth and Society, 35*(4), 452–479.

If you do not find page numbers, then add the date of access and the URL.

For an Electronic Book

When the URL is directed to finding the source, use "Available from" instead of "Retrieved from":

> Waller, A. (2008). *Constructing adolescence in fantastic realism.* Available
> from http://www.ebookstore.tandf.co.uk/html/moreinfo.
> asp?bookid=536956948

For an Electronic Chapter in a Book

> Janet, P. (1930). Autobiography of Pierre Janet. In C. Murchison (Ed.), *History
> of psychology in autobiography* (Vol. 1, pp. 123–133). Retrieved from
> http://psychclassics.yorku.ca/Janet/murchison.htm

For an Abstract

> Prus, S.G., & Gee, E. (2003). Gender differences in vulnerability to social
> determinants of health in later-life. *Canadian Journal of Public Health,
> 94*(4), 306–309. Abstract retrieved from Statistics Canada.

> Mooney, P.H. (2004). Democratizing rural economy: Institutional friction,
> sustainable struggle and the cooperative movement. *Rural Sociology,
> 69*(1). Abstract retrieved from http://www.ingenta.com

For a Curriculum Guide

> Patterson, R., Settersten, R., & Dannefer, D. (Eds.). (2007). *Life course:
> A handbook of syllabi & instructional materials.* (4th ed.). Available from
> http://www.e-noah.net/asa/asashopon-lineservice/ProductDetails.
> aspx?productID=ASAOE329L07E

For Lecture Notes

Bloom, P. (2008). *Lecture 2: Foundations: This is your brain.* [PowerPoint slides].
    Retrieved from Open Yale courses Web site: http://oyc.yale.edu/yale
    /psychology/introduction-to-psychology/content/sessions/lecture02
    .html

For Presentation Slides

Capital Community College Foundation. (1999). *Guide to grammar
    and writing clauses: Building blocks for sentences.* [PowerPoint slides].
    Retrieved from http://grammar.ccc.commnet.edu/grammar/ppt
    /clauses.pps#257,1,Clauses: Building Blocks for Sentences

For an On-line Book Review

McLaughlin, N. (2008, January 27). *Fun and games and higher education: The
    lonely crowd revisited* [Review of the book *Fun and games and higher
    education: The lonely crowd revisited*]. *The Canadian Review of Sociology.*
    Retrieved from http://www.csaa.ca/CRSA/BookReview/Reviews
    /2008REVIEWS/200801NELSEN.htm

For an On-line Movie Review

Ebert, R. (2004, Februrary 24). *The passion of the Christ* [Review of the motion
    picture *The passion of the Christ*]. Retrieved from http://www.suntimes
    .com/ebert/ebert_reviews/2004/02/022401.html

For a Bulletin and Government Document

National Center for Complementary and Alternative Medicine. (2004, Spring,
    11). Investigating the science behind plants as treatments. Retrieved
    May 24, 2004, from http://www.nccam.nih.gov/news/newsletter
    /index.htm

Voluntary Sector Initiative. Policy Development. (2003, October). Participating
    in federal public policy: A guide for the voluntary sector. Retrieved
    May 24, 2004, from http://www.vsi-isbc.ca/eng/policy/policy_guide
    /index.cfm

Canada. Parliament. House of Commons. (2004, Feb. 12). An Act to Amend
    the Contraventions Act and the Controlled Drugs and Substance Act,
    Bill C-10, Second Reading (37th Parliament, 3rd Session). Retrieved
    May 24, 2004, from http://www.parl.gc.ca/common/Bills_ls.asp?lang
    =E&Parl=37&Ses=3&ls=C10&source=Bills_House_Government

For an Article in a Printed Magazine Reproduced On-line

Wells, P. (2004, May 24). Northern Exposure. *Macleans.* Retrieved May 24,
    2004, from http://www.macleans.ca/topstories/canada/article.jsp?
    content=20040524_81280_81280

For an On-line Magazine Article with No Author

Supreme Court rules for Monsanto in key battle with Sask. farmer over seed. (2004, May 21). *Canoe*. Retrieved May 21, 2004, from http://money .canoe.ca/News/Other/2004/05/21/468178-cp.html

For an On-line Newspaper Article

Andersson, E. (2004, May 19). First time drunk, high? Likely, age 13. Globe and Mail On-line. Retrieved from http://www.globeandmail. com/servlet/story/RTGAM.20040519.wxhdrink19/BNStory/special ScienceandHealth/

3.2.6 Use the Proper Format for Audiovisual Media, Videotapes, and Television (TV) Programs

Audiovisual media (e.g., motion pictures, videotapes, and TV programs) are non-periodicals in the APA style guide. Follow the same general format as for a book reference.

Examples follow:

Davey, B., Gibson, M., McEveety, S., & Sisti, E. (Producers), & Gibson, M. (Director). (2004). *The passion of the Christ* [Motion Picture]. United States: Icon Productions.

Native land claims in BC: After 2000. [Video Recording]. (1997). Canada: CBC.

Newsworld today from Toronto. [Television broadcast]. (2008, May 19). Toronto: CBC.

On the following page is a sample references page.

Sample References Page

References

Baron, S.W. & Kennedy, L.W. (2001). Deterrence and homeless male street youths.

In Fleming et al., pp. 151–184.

Finkelstein, M. (2005). *With no direction home: Homeless youth on the road and in the streets*. Belmont, CA: Thomson Wadsworth.

Fleming, T., O'Reilly, P., & Clark, B. (Eds.) (2001). *Youth injustice: Canadian perspectives*. (2nd ed.). Toronto: Canadian Scholars' Press.

Hyde, J. (2005, April). From home to street: Understanding young people's transitions into homelessness. *J. of Adolescence, 28*(2), 171–183. doi:10.1016/j.adolescence.2005.02.001

Mayers, M. (2001). *Street kids & streetscapes*. New York: Peter Lang.

Public Health Agency of Canada. (2006, March). *Sexually transmitted infections in Canadian street youth*. Ottawa, ON: Public Health Agency of Canada.

Schaffner, L. (1999). *Teenage runaways: Broken hearts and "bad attitudes"*. Binghampton, NY: Haworth Press.

Chapter Summary

In-text citations:

- An *in-text citation* is a reference source within the text of a term paper or book review.
- You *must* use an in-text citation whenever you use another author's idea or information, including quoting, summarizing, or paraphrasing that idea or information.
- The general format for in-text citations is to present the author(s) and the year of publication. Add the page number(s) for a long work.
- Specific formatting styles are presented for print sources, which are also used for electronic sources.

References:

- *References* is the complete list of the full text of your research sources.
- Include only those reference sources that you used in your term paper or book review.
- The references page is a separate page at the end of your text that lists authors alphabetically by their last name and initials. (Where no author, use title of work.)
- To format a book reference, use the last name of the author, author initials, year of publication, title of book, place of publication, and publishing company.
- To format an article in a journal or periodical, use the last name of the author(s), author(s) initials, year of publication, title of article, name of journal or periodical, volume number and issue, and page numbers.
- To format an electronic journal source, follow the same pattern as for a print source. In addition, add the DOI if given, otherwise present the URL. Add the retrieval date when the content in a source is likely to change.
- For audiovisual media, videotapes, and TV programs, follow the same general format as for a book reference.

 Checklist for In-Text Citations and References

In-text citations

- ❏ Do you know the general meaning of an *in-text citation*?
- ❏ Do you know when to use an in-text citation?
- ❏ Do you know the general format for an in-text citation?
- ❏ Did you document all your in-text citations to avoid plagiarism?
- ❏ Do all your in-text citations, print and electronic, follow the APA formatting styles?

References

- ❏ Do you know the general meaning of *references page*?
- ❏ Do you know what to include in the list for your references page?
- ❏ Do you know the general formatting requirements for your references page list?
- ❏ Did you format your book references correctly?
- ❏ Did you format your references for articles in journals or periodicals correctly?
- ❏ Did you format your electronic sources correctly?
- ❏ Did you format your audiovisual media, videotapes, and TV programs correctly?

Recommended Web Sites

From David Warlick of The Landmark Project—an interactive Web site that will generate citations for APA, MLA, Turabian, and Chicago styles:
http://citationmachine.net/index2.php

University of Wisconsin at Madison—citing references in your paper:
http://www.wisc.edu/writing/Handbook/Documentation.html

Web site of Monash University (Australia)—some tutorials on citing and referencing:
http://www.lib.monash.edu.au/tutorials/citing/

Recommended Readings

For MLA style:

Gibaldi, J. (2009). *MLA handbook for writers of research papers.* (7th ed.). New York: The Modern Language Association of America.

For Chicago style:

Turabian, K.L. (2007). *A manual for writers of research papers, theses, and dissertations.* (7th ed.). Chicago: University of Chicago Press.

Chapter 4

Researching to Define Concepts in the Aim, Organizing Arguments, and Drafting a Conclusion

Once you have completed the first-priority items, focus on defining the concepts in the aim sentence, organizing the arguments, and drafting the conclusion to the term paper. You should add any research sources used here to your reference sources in your outline.

In this chapter you will learn to

1. define the concepts in the aim sentence,
2. organize arguments, and
3. draft a conclusion.

A sample outline for five arguments to support an aim is provided at the end of this chapter.

4.1 How Do I Define the Concepts in the Aim Sentence?

Certain words in your aim sentence will require clarification. Recall that to define a concept means clarifying the meaning of the words that present the key ideas in the aim. To assist you in providing definitions for your aim or question, follow this general process, starting with knowing which keywords or concepts to define.

4.1.1 Know Which Keywords or Concepts to Define

Not every word in the aim sentence needs to be defined. Only those words, terms, or concepts that are the main ideas in your aim must be defined.

Below are examples of aim sentences, followed by the concepts to be defined:

The aim of this paper is to demonstrate that street youth will become involved in deviant behaviour.

Reminder
Only two main ideas are used for now in creating your aim.

The concepts to be defined here are *street youth* and *deviant behaviour*.

This paper will show that street kids come from dysfunctional families.

The concepts to be defined are *street kids* and *dysfunctional families*.
Here is an example of a more complicated aim:

This paper will focus on the coping skills that street kids develop in order to survive.

The keywords or concepts to be defined are the following: *coping skills, street kids, develop*, and *survive*.

The wording of your aim is very important because you will have to define the concepts that you decide to use. You are expected to know which words are the concepts in your aim sentence that need to be defined.

4.1.2 Define the Concepts in Order

You must define the concepts in the order that they appear in the aim sentence. The first concept in the aim sentence will, therefore, be the first concept defined. The next concept in the aim sentence is defined after that. You must adhere to this order for the definitions to be consistent with the aim.

Here is an example of the order in which concepts must be defined for an aim sentence:

The aim of this paper is to demonstrate that street youth will become involved in deviant behaviour.

The concept that must be defined first is *street youth* because it appears first in the aim sentence. The concept that must be defined second is *deviant behaviour* because it appears second in the aim sentence.

The order of your definitions follows the sequence of the concepts in your aim sentence. This sequence creates consistency between your aim sentence and the definitions of your concepts. Record this order of your definitions in your outline.

4.1.3 Know That You Must Use Defined Concepts in Only One Way

A concept or keyword that you define in your aim sentence will be used in only that way. By defining a word or concept, you are restricting or limiting the meaning of that word or term (Stewart & Allen, 2005, pp. 72–73). That meaning applies to your entire term paper. That is, you must use the meaning of your concepts in the aim sentence consistently in the way that you have defined them.

To illustrate:

- Assume that your aim uses the concept *street kid* and that you define *street kid* as a homeless adolescent between the ages of 13 and 19.
- Defining the concept of *street kid* this way means that the words *street kid* can be used only that way.
- If you use the words *street kid* in any other way in your term paper (for example, to include information on someone over 19 years of age), you are using these keywords or this concept inconsistently.

Tips When your instructor reads your term paper, she or he will use your definitions to read your term paper. Your definitions are adopted or shared by the instructor reading your term paper (L. Barkley, personal communication, May 19, 2005). Your instructor will use the definitions of your concepts to determine how consistent you are in your use of them for your entire term paper.

You will run into problems if your use is inconsistent:

- If you do not use your concepts in the way that you have defined them, then your use of them is not consistent or logical. This will weaken your term paper by making it less convincing in the inconsistent parts.
- The specific argument in which your concept is used incorrectly may, in turn, weaken the understanding of your term paper's aim. Your inconsistent use may create ambiguity or doubt about your aim for your instructor.

The definitions of your concepts that you decide to use must make sense and must be applicable to your entire term paper.

4.1.4 Know That Definitions Must Come from the Course, Discipline, or Field of Studies

Your definitions of concepts or keywords must come from the course you are taking or from its field of studies. Each of these areas of study has a literature. The word *literature* is used here to mean all the writings that are part of these areas of study, including everything that has been published in books, journal articles, research reports, etc.

The definitions of your concepts must come from the particular literature in which you are writing your term paper:

- For an anthropology course, you must use the anthropology literature.
- For a psychology course, you must use the psychology literature.
- For a sociology course, you must use the sociology literature.
- For an economics course, you must use the economics literature.

There are a number of places for you to research to find definitions for the literature that you need.

4.1.5 Know Where to Research for Definitions of Concepts

Your goal in undertaking research for definitions of concepts is to record the following in your outline:

- The exact quote and reference source for the definitions
- Any additional definitions of words in your first definition

For example:

> Deviance is defined as "the recognized violation of cultural norms" (Macionis & Gerber, 2008, p. 210).

An additional concept in the preceding is *norm*, which is defined as the "rules and expectations by which a society guides the behaviour of its members" (Macionis & Gerber, 2008, p. 67).

Record both the first and additional definitions in your outline. There are a number of general areas to research for definitions of concepts, starting with textbooks.

In Textbooks

One good place to start looking for definitions is in the textbook(s) for your course, since most introductory courses have them. The definitions in your course textbook already fulfill the requirement that they are part of the literature.

Tips

You might hesitate to use a definition from your textbook that has not been discussed in class. However, most instructors would encourage you to read and use relevant textbook material not yet covered in class.

There is one word of caution concerning the use of textbooks: Do not use a definition from one course for a course of a different subject area. That is, do not use a definition from a sociology course in an economics course. A similar concept, like *socialization*, will have one definition and meaning in sociology and another definition and meaning in economics.

In Books and Articles

Another source of finding definitions of concepts in your aim is the books and articles of the relevant literature:

- The definitions of concepts in your aim will probably come from some of the books or articles that you used as the reference sources of your arguments.
- If you are unable to find definitions of concepts in these materials, then you should research other books and articles in the discipline or in the specific field of studies.
- If none of the preceding is useful, your best resource is to consult with your instructor.

In Dictionaries and Encyclopedias

Recall that there are various kinds of dictionaries and encyclopedias:

- The general community college- or university-level dictionaries (for example, *Merriam Webster Dictionary* or *Canadian Oxford Dictionary*)
- Specialized encyclopedias (for example, *Encyclopedia of Anthropology*)
- Dictionaries specializing in a discipline or field of studies (for example, dictionary of psychology or sociology)

Here are some guidelines about using the above for defining concepts:

- Use all of the above in order to understand the meaning of words and concepts.
- Do not use the general dictionaries for definitions of concepts because they present the meaning of words in everyday language and not in the professional language of the social sciences.
- Avoid using the specialized encyclopedias and dictionaries for definitions, or consult with your instructor about using them. Many instructors discourage you from using definitions from these in your term paper because they want you to be more familiar with authors and their research in a particular area and to encourage you to work with the relevant literature of your studies.

Reminder

Discuss any problems concerning definitions or meanings of the concept(s) in any of the preceding areas with your instructor.

4.2 How Do I Organize the Arguments?

Recall that to organize the arguments refers to the sequence or the order in which arguments will be made in your term paper. That is, you will state the first argument, then the second, and the third, etc. The goal here is to determine the best way to organize your arguments in support of your aim in your outline.

4.2.1 In One of Three Ways

There are at least three ways for you to arrange your arguments (Wood, 2001, pp. 300–305):

- Group similar points.
- Arrange arguments in a time sequence.
- Organize arguments in order of importance.

Group Similar Points

One way to arrange your arguments is to decide which points are similar to each other and can thus be grouped together. Begin by looking at all the points that you have listed in your outline, and pick at least two arguments that are similar to each other. Group these arguments into themes or headings. Each theme or heading might consist of a number of related arguments. Then determine the sequence in which you will present the headings or themes for arguments in your term paper.

Following are some examples of grouping similar arguments from the aim concerning street youth and their involvement in deviant behaviour. There are two points that relate to each other concerning drug use and can be grouped together:

Street kids are involved in the deviant behaviour of substance abuse.

Dealing in drugs is a deviant activity of street kids.

There are also two points related to each other concerning sexual activity; they, too, can be grouped together:

Street kids become involved in the deviant behaviour of prostitution.

Street kids are involved in the deviant behaviour of obligatory sex.

The sequence of these groups of arguments could start with drug use followed by sexual activity.

Following is an example of organizing arguments with a heading for a group of arguments, including illegal drugs and deviant sexual activity:

Street youth are highly likely to become involved in the deviant behaviour of illegal drugs, their use and dealing in them.

Street youth are also likely to become involved in deviant sexual activity, such as prostitution and obligatory sex.

Arrange Arguments in a Time Sequence

You can also organize your arguments from a starting point to an end point, or in a developmental or historical point of view. For instance, you might arrange the arguments in your term paper so that they start with becoming aware of an issue or problem and end with an argument on how to address the issue or problem.

Arranging points for street youth and their involvement in deviant behaviour could start in the following way:

- Start with the first kind of deviant behaviour that street youth become involved in.
- End with the last kind of deviant behaviour that they are likely to be involved in.

The arguments would thus be in the following possible sequence: showing that street youth start with substance abuse; move on to stealing; then begin to deal in drugs; which is followed by obligatory sex; and ends with their becoming involved in prostitution. Here is this sequence of arguments:

One kind of deviant behaviour of street kids is their involvement in substance abuse.

Once you are a street kid, you are very likely to become involved in the deviant behaviour of stealing.

Dealing in drugs is another deviant activity of street kids.

Another form of deviant behaviour that street kids engage in is obligatory sex.

Street kids also become involved in the deviant behaviour of prostitution.

Note that the wording will have to be revised when you write your term paper to show the manner in which the arguments have been organized. The arguments are organized in a time sequence (or historically, or developmentally) from the first argument to the last. Demonstrating your aim so that a sequence of time or historical development becomes apparent is one way to arrange the arguments in relation to your aim.

Organize Arguments in Order of Importance

Arguments can also be arranged according to their importance to the aim. This way of presenting arguments is more difficult because you have to make judgments about the importance of each argument to the aim. You would usually start with the second most important argument, then the third, fourth, etc., saving the most important for the last.

For example, here is what the organizing of arguments might look like based on the order of importance. You might start with the deviant behaviour that has the second highest involvement by street youth, present the rest, and end with the kind of behaviour that has the highest involvement. Here is what this way of organizing arguments might look like using the street youth example:

Once you are a street youth, you are very likely to become involved in the deviant behaviour of stealing.

Dealing in drugs is a deviant activity of street youth.

Street youth become involved in the deviant behaviour of prostitution.

Another form of deviant behaviour related to prostitution is that street youth engage in obligatory sex.

One kind of deviant behaviour of street youth is their involvement in substance abuse.

Once you have decided on which way to organize your arguments, record this arrangement of arguments in your outline. State your reason for the way you decided to organize your arguments because this is helpful to the reader, your instructor, in understanding how you are going to demonstrate your aim. Your instructor will read your arguments with this reason in mind.

4.3 How Do I Draft a Conclusion?

Recall that the word *conclusion* means the closing and end of your term paper. Although it is the end of your term paper, your conclusion is very important, especially to your aim. In your conclusion, you can remind your instructor of all the arguments that you presented to demonstrate your aim. Think of the conclusion as the final opportunity to make a convincing case for your aim sentence.

4.3.1 Know What to Include

Your conclusion should include the following:

- A restating of your aim sentence
- A summary of each argument or groups of arguments, and a reason why each argument or group supported the aim
- Recommendations for further research

Restate Your Aim Sentence

Restate your aim sentence in the past tense because you are now looking back at it. Here is an example:

> The aim of this paper was to demonstrate that street youth are very likely to be involved in deviant behaviour.

The past tense in this example is indicated by the word *was*. Using the past tense will indicate to your instructor that you are now looking back at what you have done, including the summarizing of your arguments.

Summarize Each Argument or Groups of Arguments to Show How Each Supported the Aim

There are two general parts involved in your summary:

- Summarize each argument (or groups of arguments). Follow the same sequence of arguments that you used in organizing your arguments to provide consistency and logic in your writing.
- Then, in a sentence or two, state how each argument (or group, heading, or theme) supported your aim. Your goal is to present a clear link between each argument or group of arguments and your aim in order to make your case as convincing as possible.

Here are examples for two arguments only:

1. One kind of deviant behaviour of street youth is their involvement in substance abuse.
   Supported aim—substance abuse violates laws, especially when involving street youth who are under the required age for consuming alcohol; drug usage violates laws.

2. Once you are a street youth you are very likely to become involved in the deviant behaviour of stealing.
   Supported aim—stealing violates law of private property; unacceptable behaviour in order to acquire money and property; driven to steal to support habit of substance abuse.

Make Recommendations for Further Research

It is quite acceptable to include in the conclusion any recommendations or suggestions for further research. However, keep this part short: no more than a paragraph.

Here are examples of possible ideas for further research:

- How do street youth cope by engaging in deviant behaviour?
- What happens to street youth as they transition from youth into adulthood?
- What kinds of policies and services might help them?

Reminder
To help guide you when you write, make sure that you record in your outline these various aspects of drafting a conclusion.

4.3.2 Consult with Your Instructor

You should now have a completed outline. There are still, however, some final additional things that you need to find out from your instructor based on your previous consultation:

- Are the definitions of concepts appropriate?
- Does the organization of arguments make sense?
- Is the conclusion fitting for the aim?
- Is the outline complete?

Again, incorporate your instructor's comments into revising your outline before you proceed to write your term paper. Following is an example of an outline for a starting social science term paper that has five arguments to support an aim. Please note the following about this outline:

- A title page has been omitted.
- Some extra information and formatting has been added to help clarify the decisions made in the development of the outline.
- Some additional evidence beyond the suggested two or three has been included. This additional evidence allows you to see patterns or trends for each point.
- The references page and the individual references will need to be formatted using APA style once the term paper is written. At present, all information that is necessary for each research source is included.

Sample Outline

The First Social Science Outline

General topic: teen runaways; street kids (alcohol abuse; FASD—these extra topics were not required because there was enough available information on teen runaways and street kids)

Aim: what will be demonstrated

For introduction to aim sentence *(from unused portions of arguments)*:

U.S. runaway population estimates are 58 per cent female, 42 per cent male (U.S. Department Fact Sheet, 1990 in Schaffner, 1999, p. 21).

The national average age of runaways is 15 years (NASW, 1993 in Schaffner, 1999, p. 21).

Canada does not appear to have any official data.

U.S. ethnic/racial backgrounds of runaway teens are: 69–70 per cent white; 7 per cent Latino/Puerto Rican; 17–20 per cent African-American; 4 per cent other combined (Burgess, 1986, and USGAO, 1989, in Schaffner, 1999, p. 21).

Majority (58 per cent) of teen runaways are from "homes that were disadvantaged economically", for example, on "low-paying, unskilled occupations or public assistance for parents" (Schaffner, 1999, p. 21).

Street kids:

Street kids are involved in panhandling or begging. Panhandling means asking passersby for money ("spare change") or food (Finkelstein, 2005, p. 73).

Girls get more money than boys because they are girls (Finkelstein, 2005, p. 75).

Panhandling was the main source of money (Finkelstein, 2005, p. 73); money was for beer, not food, which was easier to get (Finkelstein, 2005, pp. 67–68).

Street kids were humiliated by passersby (Finkelstein, 2005, p. 73).

Violence among street kids was mostly due to alcohol and drug intoxication.

Most kids carried a weapon—a knife or a "smiley (large lock and chain used to hit people)" (Finkelstein, 2005, p. 107).

Knife fights on street were guided more by "impulse and emotion" than careful planning (Baron & Kennedy, 2001, p. 172).

Alcohol was given as the main reason for close friends on streets who fight with each other (Finkelstein, 2005, p. 109).

A significant aspect to investigating teen runaways, street kids, homeless youth, street youth was no consensus on use of these words and their meaning.

Aim sentence:

The aim of this paper is to demonstrate that street youth are very likely to be involved in deviant behaviour.

Aim sentence worded as a question:

In what kinds of deviant behaviour are street youth likely to be involved?

Define concepts (concepts from the aim that will be defined and from their sources):

The two main concepts from the aim that need to be defined are *street youth* and *deviant behaviour*.

Street youth:

Here is why the concept *street youth* was chosen instead of *teen runaways* or *street kids*.

The following three definitions were examined:

1. *Teen runaways*

   Teen runaways is defined as "youths under the age of eighteen who absent themselves from home or place of legal residence at least overnight without permission of parents or legal guardians" (U.S. General Accounting Office, 1989; National Network of Runaway and Youth Services, 1991 in Schaffner, 1999, p. 21).

2. *Street kids*

   Street kids is defined as kids of a young age, and who are absent from home "without a parent's permission, usually for 24 hours or more" (Shane, 1996, in Mayers, 2001, p. 139).

   Another definition: Finkelstein (2005) defines *street kids* "(and the alternative terms, *homeless adolescents* or *homeless youth*) as young people under the age of 21 who have separated themselves from their families (whether by parental consent or not) and now live entirely on the streets (i.e., not in shelters)" (p. 3).

3. *Street youth*

   Street youth are a) between 15 and 24 years, b) able to speak English or French, c) had in previous six months, either been absent from their residence for at least three consecutive nights, or run away from home (or another place of residence) for three days or more, or been thrown out of their home for three days or more, or been without a fixed address for three days or more (Public Health Agency of Canada [PHAC], 2006, p. 3).

From the three preceding definitions (teen runaways, street kids, street youth):

There is overlap in comparing all three definitions and hence difficult to separate teen runaways, homeless kids, and youth living on street.

The word *street* is used to refer to being homeless or of no fixed address.

The age range from the definitions is from under 18 to 24 (i.e., 15–24 years).

The time away from home or residence, being absent, ranged from overnight to three or more days.

Here is the wording of the definition of *street youth* and the reason for this decision:

For this term paper, a street youth is defined as a homeless person under 24 years of age who is absent without permission from overnight to three or more days.

The reason for choosing *street youth* was so that all research data from the reference sources that is used as evidence in the arguments could be included.

This decision resulted in a change of wording in the aim sentence from *street kids* to *street youth*.

Deviant behaviour:

Deviance is defined as "the recognized violation of cultural norms" (Macionis & Gerber, 2008, p. 210).

The word *norm* in this definition refers to the "rules and expectations by which a society guides the behaviour of its members" (Macionis & Gerber, 2008, p. 67).

Specifically, the emphasis of the aim is on "proscriptive norms", which is defined as "what we should not do" (Macionis & Gerber, 2008, p. 67).

Restating the definition:

Deviance refers to the kind of behaviour that defies what members of a society consider acceptable and what should not be done.

Street youth and deviant behaviour:

Here are examples of stating the aim by using the meanings of the preceding definitions:

Homeless youth will become involved in behaviour that defies the rules and expectations of their society.

Street youth will behave in ways that members of their society consider unacceptable.

Organize arguments *(the sequence of five arguments)*:

The arguments have been organized according to street youth's greatest to least involvement in deviant behaviour:

1. One kind of deviant behaviour of street youth is their involvement in substance abuse.
2. Once you are a street youth you are very likely to become involved in the deviant behaviour of stealing.
3. Dealing in drugs is a deviant activity of street youth.
4. Street youth become involved in the deviant behaviour of prostitution.
5. Another form of deviant behaviour related to prostitution is that street youth engage in obligatory sex.

Presentation of arguments *(the points and evidence to support each point)*:

1. Point or (Point 1): One kind of deviant behaviour of street youth is their involvement in substance abuse.

Substance abuse and use includes alcohol and illegal drugs.

Evidence:

Substance abuse as high as 94 per cent in a homeless youth sample (Russel, 1998, in Mayers, 2001, p. 155).

Drug or alcohol abuse as high as 84 per cent (from a sample of 50) (Finkelstein, 2005, p. 86).

98 per cent drank alcohol; 62 per cent smoked marijuana; 50 per cent did cocaine; 24 per cent, speed; 30 per cent LSD; and 72 per cent shot heroine (Finkelstein, 2005, p. 86); Ecstasy rarely mentioned, possibly due to high cost (Finkelstein, 2005, p. 68).

Needle sharing and risk of HIV or hepatitis C from sample was 72 per cent who used needles to inject drugs and 57 per cent shared needles, thus increasing risk of getting HIV, hepatitis C, and other blood diseases (Finkelstein, 2005, p. 97).

Sharing drug paraphernalia (for example, needles) for possible HIV transmission was roughly 33 per cent for both females and males (Rosenthal, Moore & Buzwell, 1994, in Mayers, 2001, p. 156).

2. Point or (Point 2): Once you are a street youth you are very likely to become involved in the deviant behaviour of stealing.

Stealing or theft includes shoplifting, boosting (stealing merchandise from one store and selling it to another), and scams (conning people) (Finkelstein, 2005, p. 81).

Evidence:

60 per cent admitted to petty crimes, for example, stealing in hospitals (Finkelstein, 2005, p. 81); scams, for example, fake drug deals—just take money and never return with the drugs (Finkelstein, 2005, pp. 82–83).

The less certain that street youth were of punishment and the lower the severity or the punishment, the more houses and cars they broke into (Baron & Kennedy, 2001, p. 167).

As time spent on street increases, so does criminal activity and severity of crimes; all types of crimes increased after more than 12 months (McCarthy & Hagan, 2001, p. 150).

3. Point or (Point 3): Dealing in drugs is a deviant activity of street youth.

Dealing drugs refers to selling illegal drugs in order to make money, primarily to support their habit (Finkelstein, 2005, p. 79).

Evidence:

From 40 to 50 per cent of kids sold, ran, or moved drugs (drug dealing) (Finkelstein, 2005, p. 79).

Make over five times their investment from acid, for example, buy for $100 a sheet and sell up to $500 a sheet (Finkelstein, 2005, p. 80).

4. Point or (Point 4): Street youth become involved in the deviant behaviour of prostitution.

Prostitution includes not only sex for money.

Sometimes prostitution for street youth is referred to as "survival sex", that is, "sex in exchange for money, food, or shelter" (Mayers, 2001, p. 152).

Similar to survival sex is Public Health Agency of Canada's (PHAC) definition of *sex trade*, which is the "exchange of sexual activities to meet subsistence needs such as food, shelter and protection" (PHAC, 2006, p. 19).

Rationale—best way to make a lot of money fast (Finkelstein, 2005, p. 76) or last resort to get money quickly (Finkelstein, 2005, p. 78).

Evidence:

18 per cent admitted to prostitution (under-reported) (Finkelstein, 2005, p. 76).

35 per cent engaged in some type of sexual favours in exchange for either money or shelter (Finkelstein, 2005, p. 75).

44.4 per cent of Aboriginal youth who do run away become involved in prostitution (Schissel & Fedec, 2001, p. 138).

The average was 21.2 per cent of street youth who were involved in sex trade (PHAC, 2006, p. 19).

5. Point or (Point 5): Final form of deviant behaviour related to prostitution is that street youth engage in obligatory sex.

> The meaning of *obligatory sex* is "having sex when obligated to do so after having received money, gifts, drugs, or a place to sleep" (PHAC, 2006, p. 20).

> May also include *unwanted sex*, meaning "having sex but not wanting to do so with someone in a position of authority" (PHAC, 2006, p. 19).

Evidence:

> The obligatory sex average was 18.5 per cent. Street youth reported feeling obligated to have sex at some time; females more likely than males—25.5 per cent vs. 14.3 per cent (PHAC, 2006, p. 20).

> Kinds of obligatory sex included shelter (38 per cent), cigarettes, drugs and/or alcohol (33.2 per cent), and money (25.9 per cent) (PHAC, 2006, p. 20).

> From 1999 to 2002, around 18 per cent average for unwanted sex (PHAC, 2006, p. 19).

> Percentage of female youth experiencing unwanted sex was more than double that of males. The difference was significant: between 1999 and 2002, the average was 27.5 per cent (females) vs. 12 per cent (males) (PHAC, 2006, p. 19).

Conclusion (restate aim and how each argument supported the aim):

(Restate aim sentence in past tense): The aim of this paper was to demonstrate that street youth are very likely to be involved in deviant behaviour.

1. *Argument:* One kind of deviant behaviour of street youth was their involvement in substance abuse.
   Supported aim—substance abuse violates laws, especially for street youth who are under the required age for consuming alcohol.
2. *Argument:* Once you are a street youth you are very likely to become involved in the deviant behaviour of stealing.
   Supported aim—stealing is a property crime and is a criminal offence, possibly driven to steal to support habit of substance abuse.
3. *Argument:* Dealing in drugs was a deviant activity of street youth.
   Supported aim—selling illegal drugs violates laws; perpetuates unacceptable behaviour of use of drugs.
4. *Argument:* Street youth became involved in the deviant behaviour of prostitution.
   Supported aim—prostitution violates accepted behaviour of romantic and free love; violates criminal laws.
5. *Argument:* Another form of deviant behaviour related to prostitution was that street youth engage in obligatory sex.
   Supported aim—obligatory sex violates the expectation that a favour is done out of kindness, now there is an expectation of payment or reward involved and that is sex.

Future questions:

How do street youth cope by engaging in deviant behaviour?

What happens to street youth as they transition from youth into adulthood?

What kinds of policies and services might help them?

References (APA style: list all books, periodicals, and other references)

(Note that the library call numbers have been added in case the books are needed after they have been returned; that all sources may not be used in writing the term paper; and that the references page will need to be formatted, as per APA style, after term paper is written.)

Baron, S.W., & Kennedy, L.W. (2001). Deterrence and homeless male street youths. In Fleming et al., pp. 151–184.

Finkelstein, M. (2005). With no direction home: Homeless youth on the road and in the streets. Belmont, CA: Thomson Wadsworth. [HV 1437 N5 F56 2005]

Fleming, T., O'Reilly, P., & Clark, B. (Eds.) (2001). Youth injustice: Canadian perspectives. (2nd ed.). Toronto: Canadian Scholars' Press. [KE 9445 Y69 2001]

Hyde, J. (2005, April). From home to street: Understanding young people's transitions into homelessness. J. of Adolescence, 28(2), 171–183. doi:10.1016/j.adolescence.2005.02.001

Macionis, J.J., & Gerber, L.M. (2008). Sociology. Toronto: Pearson/Prentice Hall.

Mayers, M. (2001). Street kids & streetscapes. N.Y.: Peter Lang. [HV 1431 M36 2001]

Public Health Agency of Canada. (March 2006). Sexually transmitted infections in Canadian street youth. Ottawa, ON: Public Health Agency of Canada. [RA 644 V4 S48 2006]

Schaffner, L. (1999). Teenage runaways: Broken hearts and "bad attitudes". Binghampton, N.Y.: Haworth Press. [HV1431 S35 1999]

Schissel, B., & Fedec, K. (2001). The selling of innocence: The gestalt of danger in the lives of youth prostitutes. In Fleming et al., pp. 125–149.

Webber, M. (1991). Street kids: The tragedy of Canada's runaways. Toronto: U. of Toronto. [HQ 799 C2 W42 1991]

Chapter Summary

Define the concepts in the aim sentence:

- Define keywords or concepts in aim sentence.
- Define concepts in the same order as the aim sentence.
- You must use defined concepts in only one way.
- You must use definitions from the course, discipline, or field of studies.
- Research definitions of concepts in textbooks, books, and articles.
- Use dictionaries and encyclopedias to help you understand concepts only.

Organize the arguments:

Organize arguments in the following ways: group similar points; arrange in a time sequence; arrange in order of importance.

Draft a conclusion:

Include the following in your conclusion:

- A restating of your aim sentence
- A summary of each argument or group of arguments in the same sequence as the order of your arguments
- A reason why each argument or group of arguments supported the aim
- Some recommendations for further research

Consult with your instructor about your completed outline.

Checklist for Term Paper Research

Define the concepts in the aim sentence:

- ☐ Do you know which keywords or concepts to define in the aim sentence?
- ☐ Did you define the concepts in the same order as the aim sentence?
- ☐ Do you know that defined concepts can be used in only one way?
- ☐ Did your definitions come from the course, discipline, or field of studies?
- ☐ Did you do research for definitions of concepts in textbooks, books, and articles?
- ☐ Did you record the definitions and their reference sources in your outline?

Organize the arguments:

- ❑ Did you organize the arguments in your outline?
- ❑ What was the reason for organizing your arguments in the way that you did?

Drafting a conclusion:

- ❑ Did you restate your aim sentence?
- ❑ Did you summarize each argument or group of arguments in the same sequence as the order of your arguments?
- ❑ Did you give a reason why each argument or group of arguments supported the aim?
- ❑ What kinds of recommendations for further research did you make?
- ❑ Did you consult with your instructor about your completed outline —what comments were made, and did you revise your completed outline?

Recommended Web Sites

The OWL at Purdue University—on organizing an argument following the Toulmin Method of logic:

http://owl.english.purdue.edu/owl/resource/588/03/#resourcenav/

University of Wollongong, Australia—UniLearning Web site on identifying concepts:

http://unilearning.uow.edu.au/essay/2b.html

The Writing Center, University of North Carolina at Chapel Hill—on writing conclusions beyond the beginning level:

http://www.unc.edu/depts/wcweb/handouts/conclusions.html

Recommended Readings

On organizing arguments and drafting a conclusion:

Booth, W.C., Colomb, G.G., & Williams, J.M. (2008). *The craft of research.* Chicago: University of Chicago Press.

Norton, S., & Green, B. (2006). *Essay essentials.* (4th ed.). Scarborough, ON: Thomson/Nelson.

Chapter 5
Writing the First Social Science Term Paper

Once you have completed your research outline on your computer, you should do the following:

- Make sure that you have made a full backup copy of your completed research outline on a separate storage device.
- Print one or two copies of your completed research outline: one copy for you and one for your instructor, if required.

You have completed your research outline, where you used inductive thinking. Now, you need to write a coherent term paper where you will use deductive thinking to present your research. You will use deductive thinking to write your term paper because you will convey your general aim before you present your specific arguments in support of your aim.

This chapter will present the various aspects of writing your term paper. They include the following steps:

1. Write a term paper draft.
2. Revise the draft.
3. Format the term paper.
4. Write the abstract (if required).
5. Create a title page.
6. Produce the final copy.

5.1 How Do I Write a Term Paper Draft?

You should prepare to write the draft of your term paper by doing the following:

- Make a copy of your research outline to create a new file that you will now use to write your term paper draft.
- Make a backup copy of your new term paper draft file on a separate storage device (for example, USB flash drive), and update your backup copy regularly as you write.

This section will help you write a better term paper draft by presenting some introductory writing skills. Follow these recommendations or consult your instructor on items not mentioned here.

5.1.1 Use Required Writing Skills

The Introduction to this book presented some required writing skills for a social science term paper. This section adds to the list of skills and encourages you to *double-check* for any of the following errors.

Spelling

All of the words in your term paper must be spelled correctly. Use a dictionary to assist you in your writing.

There are some aspects of spelling that cause problems for beginning students. They include abbreviations, acronyms, capitalization, and numbers. Following are some brief suggestions on how deal with each.

An *abbreviation* is a shorter version of a word, phrase, or term that contains periods.

For example:

Before the common era (BCE)

In general, as a beginning writer you should avoid using abbreviations. Instead, write your intended abbreviations out in full. The reason for this is that your writing will be clearer and you are more likely to use the full words correctly:

- Do not use *e.g.* Write out *for example.*
- Do not abbreviate days, months, and holidays. (For example, do not use *Xmas*; write out *Christmas.*)

There are, however, some generally accepted abbreviations that you do not necessarily have to write out first:

- Some large institutions
  Examples:
  SFU, MIT

- Commonly referred to organizations
  Examples:
  CIA, UN

- Large corporations
  Examples:
  MSN, RIM

- Some countries
  Examples:
  U.S.A. (USA) or U.S. (US)

If you are unsure about using a common abbreviation, use the following guideline: write out the full words or terms that you are abbreviating the first time that they are used, and put their abbreviations in parentheses after the term.

Example:

fetal alcohol syndrome (F.A.S.)

An *acronym* is an abbreviation that spells a pronounceable word that does not contain periods. Acronyms are used so often that you do not have to write out what they stand for.

Examples:

WHO

NATO

NASA

Again, if you are unsure about any of the preceding then follow the previous guideline of writing out the words followed by their abbreviation or acronym in parentheses.

For those using a word-processing program, you will need to learn to work with your AutoCorrect function. For uppercase letters, you may want to turn this function off so that it does not capitalize words unnecessarily. In general, it is a good idea to turn off any automatic style or formatting function. If you are unsure about capitalizing a certain word, look up the word in a recent dictionary.

As well, there are different ways to write numbers for your term paper. Two general ways are to write out the numbers or to use the figure for the number:

1. Write the word for the number when it is part of the general use for your term paper.
   Example:

   My first argument is . . .

2. Use the figure for the number, unless it begins a sentence (in which case you would write the word), for other purposes.
   Example:

   There were 23 runaway teens last year.

In some instances either numbers or words are acceptable.

Example:

From 2011 to 2015 [*or* 2011–2015] . . .

The court awarded damages of one million dollars. [*or* The court awarded damages of $1,000,000.]

Finally, *avoid* using verbal contractions in your writing such as *didn't* instead of *did not*. Writing out these negations will help you avoid the potential use of double negatives.

All of the preceding should help you to write a term paper with correct spelling and usage.

Grammar

You must write your term paper using correct grammar. As you are writing, make sure that your sentences adhere to the following grammar basics presented in the Introduction to this book:

- Singular and plural agreement
- Correct group use
- Correct verb tense
- Clear pronoun reference
- Grammatically parallel sentences

One general area of grammar to note here is the correct use of verb tense in your draft:

- For the organization of arguments portion, use the future verb tense.
  Why? Because in this section you refer to arguments that you will present in a certain order.
- For the conclusion, use the past verb tense.
  Why? Because in this section you are writing about what you have presented.

Punctuation

The punctuation in your term paper must be exact. When writing your draft, it is worth repeating the following: keep your sentences simple, which will simplify your use of correct punctuation.

One particular area of concern for punctuation is where to put quotation marks. Standard North American practice is to put all punctuation inside the quotation marks (see p. 164). An alternative practice follows these guidelines:

- If the end punctuation is part of a quote, then put the *quotation marks after* it. Example:

  The runaway teen said, "Where will I live?"

- If the end punctuation is *not* part of the quote, then put the *quotation marks before* it.
  Example:

  The researcher was not sure what caused the runaway teen to say, "I knew exactly where I would go".

- When a *quotation occurs within a quotation*, use *single quotation marks* (' '). Example:

  The researcher said, "I heard you say, 'I will never go home again.'"

Whichever practice you adopt, be sure to follow it consistently throughout your paper.

Quotations

This section will offer some brief suggestions on the use of quoting in your research paper.

It is better to integrate a quote into your sentence:

Example of original quote:

> "Psychologists have made great strides in understanding the addictive personality," maintains Smith.

Example of original quote integrated into your sentence:

> Smith argues that significant advances have been made by psychologists in "understanding the addictive personality".

Reminder

All quotes from an author must be referenced properly (see Chapter 3 for details).

Once you have presented your quote, then *clarify* what the quote means and *elaborate* on how these words relate to what you are writing about. This process will make your use of a quote clear and relevant to what you are writing about.

In addition, here are two things to avoid in quoting: long quotes and stringing quotes.

Limit the length of quotes in your term paper.

Avoid long quotes such as those that fill an entire page. Your term paper should make sense when a lengthy quote is omitted. Your quote should support your argument instead of making it for you!

Instead of using a long quote, *paraphrase* the author's idea. Paraphrasing demonstrates to your instructor than you can competently summarize and use the idea or point from an author's work to support your argument.

Do not string one quote after another.

Inserting one quote after another makes it difficult to understand what you are saying. Instead, present the first quote and how it supports your argument, then present your second quote and what it means for your argument, and so on. Remember, each quote requires that you state its source or author, year, and page number.

Appropriate Language

In addition to using these required writing skills, avoid words and language that are sexist or bigoted. Instead, use non-sexist, non-racist, and non-derogatory words. As well, avoid using local phrasing, slang, or swear words as well as metaphors. Remember that this is a *formal* social science term paper.

Reminder

Remember to write in a *neutral tone* even though you are writing an argumentative term paper. To write in a neutral tone means to use words, phrases, and evidence that present your view(s) in a factual and reasonable manner. Avoid writing in a highly emotional or arrogant style.

5.1.2 Use Proper Sentences, Paragraphs, and Transitions

This section will help you write a draft of your term paper. To do this, you must write your term paper draft as follows:

- In the same order as the headings of your basic social science argumentative format and process
- By including all parts of your research outline
- By adding to your research outline (such as adding an introduction to your aim sentence)

It is worth repeating that all parts of your social science term paper must be written in complete sentences and proper paragraphs. Connecting the ideas from one sentence to the next or from one paragraph to the next is referred to as a *transition*. You can use a word, phrase, or sentence to connect sentences, and to connect paragraphs.

Reminder
- The goal of your writing is to create a *coherent* and *unified* term paper.
- Do *not* submit a term paper to your instructor that consists merely of unrelated parts.

Here, we temporarily use the headings of the basic social science argumentative format and process so that you will know where to use the suggestions for sentences, paragraphs, and transitions. You must delete these headings in your draft, except References, unless your instructor directs you to do otherwise.

Tips   Delete the basic social science argumentative format and process headings as you work on a particular part of your term paper.

Introduction to Aim

The introduction to your aim should generally consist of one to two paragraphs. These paragraphs might include the following:

- Important background or historical information leading up to your aim sentence
- The significance and importance of your aim
- The current relevance of your aim

Writing the first sentence for your introduction may be generally intimidating. Here are some possibilities for first sentences:

One of the main areas of interest within the topic of (*fill in general area of aim*) is this.

The (*insert your topic*) did not develop suddenly. It developed in the following general way.

What makes (*fill in general area of aim*) important is this.

Your introductory sentences and paragraphs should lead naturally to your aim sentence.

Transition to aim sentence.
Here are some suggestions for the transition to your aim sentence:

The preceding discussion has highlighted the importance of (*fill in general area of aim*). (*Present your aim.*)

The significance of this (*topic/aim/issue*) suggests the following. The aim of this paper is . . .

The controversy of this debate continues, and the term paper will present the following aim.

Aim Sentence

As a beginning student, you should keep your aim to one brief sentence or question that should appear toward the end of your introduction.

Here are some suggestions for wording your aim sentence:

The aim of this paper is to demonstrate . . .

The thesis of this paper is . . .

The question that this term paper addresses is this: . . .

Notice that these sentences clearly state that this is your aim sentence or question. There should be no doubt what the aim of your paper is. Do not write an aim sentence or question that contains only one concept instead of the required two. Also, avoid having three or more concepts in your aim for now so that your task is more manageable.

Transition from aim to definitions.
Here are some possible transitions that you might use to connect the aim sentence to definitions of the concepts in your aim:

In order to clarify the aim of this paper, the following definitions are presented.

The concepts in the aim sentence are defined as follows.

The aim sentence is going to be elaborated on by defining these concepts.

Definition of Concepts in Aim

You can usually write the definitions of the concepts in your aim sentence in one or two paragraphs. The order of the definitions is generally as follows:

- The concept that is defined first is the one that appears first in your aim sentence.
- The second concept will be the second one in your aim sentence, and so on.

Here is the general pattern that you should use in writing a definition for a concept in your aim:

- State that you are presenting the first concept from your aim.

Example:

> The concept is . . .

- Present the definition of the concept, usually another author's, place it in quotation marks, and cite it appropriately.
- Then state what the words of the definition mean in your own words.
- Now, state how the definition relates to your aim.

After you present the first definition in this way, you will need a transition to your next definition:

Example:

> The next concept in the aim is . . .

Then repeat the previous pattern starting by giving the definition of the second concept. It is vital that you use references for your definitions from your research. These reference citations are important to your instructor because it shows that you are using the language of the discipline or field of studies in your term paper. It also shows that you are aware of other authors and their research, and are able to use their work to support your writing.

Reminder
- Define only the two concepts in your aim.
- Do not define any additional words that are not used in the aim sentence. Define them where they are used in the text of your term paper.

Restate your aim sentence using the definitions of your concepts. This will help to clarify what your aim means.

Transition from definitions to organization of arguments.

Use a transition after you have finished defining the concepts in your aim to indicate that you are now going to write about the order in which you will present your arguments.

Examples:

> Having defined the concepts of the aim, the next section will present the order of the arguments.

> The concepts of the aim and how they will be used have been clarified. The next aspect of this term paper presents the sequence of arguments that will be made in support of the aim.

Organization of Arguments

Write this part of your first term paper in a paragraph. Writing this section clearly will help guide your instructor on which argument leads off and which one is last—just like a table of contents or a menu.

You should present your arguments in general terms here because you will be going into more detail for each argument later. In general, you should do the following:

- Provide the two main concepts or terms of your aim in each argument.
- Use the future tense because you are referring to arguments that you *will* present.

Here are some suggestions for the wording of your arguments, concerning their sequence:

> The first argument will be . . .
>
> The next argument will be . . .
>
> This is followed by . . .
>
> A further argument that will be made is . . .
>
> The final argument that will be presented is . . .

Note the use of *variety* in the wording of transitions here. Do *not* simply state "The first argument will be," "The second argument will be," "The third argument will be," and so on. Such writing would clearly lack interest.

As well, do not merely list the arguments you will make. Write them in proper sentences and in a paragraph to gain experience doing this. In future papers, as the number of your arguments increases, you will be able to write proper sentences about groups of arguments in headings or themes.

Tips | Do not refer to an example, clarify a point, or define a term used in an argument. Present this kind of information later in your term paper.

Transition from organization of arguments to presentation of arguments.

You need a transition to indicate that you are now changing from the organization of arguments to their presentation.

Suggestions for transitions here include the following:

> Having presented the sequence of arguments, the next part of this term paper will present the actual arguments.
>
> This part of the term paper stated how the arguments in support of the aim have been organized. The next aspect will present these arguments in their prearranged order.

Presentation of Arguments

State that the arguments to support the aim will be presented next. Some examples include the following:

> The first argument is . . .
>
> The first argument demonstrating the aim is . . .
>
> To begin, the first argument is . . .

Presentation of the point of an argument.

State one point and clarify it in a paragraph. You can clarify your point in a number of ways:

- Define a particular concept in your point, and write the definition in your own words.
- You can also include synonyms for certain words.
- Restate your point in the other terminology that you have introduced.

The elaboration of your point should be absolutely clear. The order that you clarify words in the point should follow the order that they appear in your point. (This is the same pattern that you used in defining the concepts in the aim sentence.) The first word clarified is the word that is used first in your point sentence, then the second, etc.

Summarize your clarifications and write what they mean for the point that you are presenting. Elaborating on your point like this will give more meaning to your evidence.

Reminder

- *A one-sentence point without any clarification is unacceptable.* Clarifying the words of your point will help to make your point clear. It will also help your instructor understand the point that you are writing about.
- Do not present more than one point for each argument because each point will require evidence or proof.

Tips

If you are concerned about what to do with *history* or background information on a topic, include it in your introduction or make it into an argument. If neither of these options works for you, omit history or background from your term paper.

Transition from point to evidence.

It is important to have a transition to indicate that you are presenting evidence in support of your point.

Example:

The evidence to support (*restate your point*) is . . .

One example of (*restate your point*) is the following.

Presentation of Evidence in Support of Your Point

You should provide the evidence for a point in a separate paragraph because you are presenting something different. A different paragraph helps keep the tasks of presenting a point and its evidence separate for now. Separating the evidence in another paragraph from the point also makes it easier for the instructor to follow what you are writing.

Some examples of presenting evidence after your transition might start as follows:

> The example here is . . .
>
> The statistic is . . .
>
> The research indicates . . .
>
> The information gathered by . . .

Reminder

You need to present only one clear finding of your point. Remember, do not present more than two or three pieces of evidence for a point for now, nor provide long, detailed descriptions and thus fail to specify the point with the evidence that you are providing. Shorten descriptions that are more than one paragraph.

Transition from one argument to another argument.

Once you have completed an argument, you will need a transition to the next argument. Some examples of transition sentences for you to use are as follows:

> In addition to the preceding argument . . .
>
> An additional argument is that . . .
>
> Furthermore, there is the point . . .
>
> The final argument addressing the aim of this term paper is that . . .

Transition from argument to conclusion.

Once your arguments have ended, you will need a transition to indicate that you are ending your term paper. Here are some examples of possible transitions:

> The preceding argument was the last one offered in support of the aim. Here is how all the arguments supported the aim.
>
> This was the last argument. The term paper will end by summarizing how the previous arguments supported the aim.

Conclusion

Write a couple of paragraphs to end your term paper. The format for your conclusion should generally be this:

- Begin the conclusion by restating your aim in the past tense.
- Then briefly summarize each argument (or group of arguments) in the past tense and state how each supported your aim.

One way to start is to introduce your conclusion with a sentence such as the following:

> In conclusion, this paper has demonstrated that (*restate your aim here*).
>
> In summary, the aim of this paper was (*restate your aim here*).

This sentence signals to your instructor that what follows is the conclusion of your term paper. Present the same sequence of arguments in summary form as you did in your term paper:

- Start with a summary of each argument in a sentence or two.
- Then present a sentence or two of how each argument supported the aim. Do not omit any one of these.
- Avoid presenting a summary argument and how it supported the aim in one sentence. Use separate sentences for now until you gain some experience in writing a summary.

Do not include any new points, definitions, or examples in your conclusion. Your term paper is essentially finished, with the exception of the references. As you gain experience in writing, your conclusions will include restating the aim and summarizing how various groups of arguments (headings, subheadings, or themes) supported the aim. You may also wish to suggest, in a paragraph, further work in the area that you are writing about.

Once you are done writing your draft, make sure that you have *deleted these basic social science argumentative format and process headings* (unless directed otherwise by your instructor).

References

Follow and use the APA style (see Chapter 3), and avoid making errors in the use of the APA style, such as leaving out the city of a published book. You must provide the complete reference. Include only those references that you *actually used* in writing your term paper.

Reminder

- Do not number your references.
- Always include sources in your term paper. Otherwise, you do not really have a research paper.
- Avoid having too few references, i.e., fewer than your instructor requires. Using too few sources indicates to your instructor that you did not do enough research on the topic. Your term paper then does not have enough research supporting your aim and arguments.

5.1.3 Consult Your Instructor

Once you have completed the previous portion and any other directions from your instructor, you will have a draft of your social science term paper. Before revising your draft term paper, you should consult with your instructor one final time about your draft. Your instructor's suggestions or recommendations must be included when revising your draft term paper.

5.2 How Do I Revise My Draft?

Before you revise the draft copy of your term paper it is a good idea to do the following:

- Set the draft aside for a day or two.
- Read your work out loud.
- Find someone with more writing experience and familiarity with the subject to read and check your work before you hand it in.

Wondering how your term paper might be evaluated? There are at least two general ways—completeness and individual criteria.

Completeness: Do you have all the required parts?	Individual Criteria: How well did you do on each part and on overall coherence?
• Abstract (if required) • Introduction and aim sentence • Definition of concepts • Organization of arguments • Presentation of arguments • Conclusion • In-text citations • References	• Writing skills • Abstract (if required) • Introduction and aim sentence • Definition of concepts • Organization of arguments • Presentation of arguments • Conclusion • In-text citations • References

Note: Your instructor may change, delete, or add to these minimum criteria.

Then, proofread your draft. To *proofread* means to read your paper again, checking for any errors. When proofreading, you should check for the following:

- Clear use of words and basic writing skills—replace redundant words and use variety for overused words.
- Neutral tone in your writing.
- That all required parts are included—there are no missing parts, from introduction to references page.
- Coherent and consistent writing—your writing is logical and deals with each idea or thought in its proper sequence, using transitions.
- Clear and effective arguments—each point and supporting evidence relates to each other and is convincing.
- Unified term paper—your writing relates clearly every idea, paragraph, or part of the term paper.

Remember that virtually all instructors will evaluate basic writing abilities as part of the term paper. Proofreading your work is essential. As well, you should make sure that you have formatted your term paper properly.

5.3 How Do I Format My Term Paper?

To format your term paper refers to its appearance. There are certain APA style rules about what your term paper should look like. The following items are general standards for formatting your term paper (some are repeated briefly for your convenience):

- Use standard letter-size paper.
- Use one side of the page only.
- Use one-inch margins.
- Use 12-point font size.
- Use Times New Roman font.
- For abstract (if required), centre the word *Abstract* at the top of the page, and do not indent first line.
- For references page, centre the word *References* at the top of the page, place all references in correct alphabetical sequence, and indent second and any additional lines a half-inch.

Reminder
See sample references page in Chapter 3.

- For quotations over 40 words, single-space as a block of text and indent the entire quote a half-inch with no quotation marks.
- Double-space rest of term paper, including the abstract and the references page.

If your instructor requires any changes to these items, you must follow those directions.

5.4 How Do I Write an Abstract?

Some instructors may require you to write an abstract of your term paper, while others may not. If required, this section will help you write an abstract, which is a brief summary of your term paper on a separate page following the title page.

The abstract must include the manuscript page header in the top-right corner (including the page number: *ii*) as well as the following:

- The word *abstract* must be capitalized (Abstract) and placed at the top of the page and centred.
- The abstract cannot be more than 120 words.
- The abstract is typed as one paragraph with no indention for the first line.
- The abstract is double-spaced.

Follow this order for your abstract:

- State the importance or significance of your aim sentence.
- State the aim or purpose of your term paper.
- End with a summary of your arguments as conclusions in support of your aim.

Consult journals or periodicals in your specific discipline or field of studies for examples of abstracts.

5.5 What Should the Title Page Look Like?

The title page is a separate page with all items centred (except the manuscript page header) and double-spaced. You have already recorded your instructor's requirements for a title page at the outset of this assignment (see Introduction).

Here is an example of requirements for a title page, and an example of what your title page should look like:

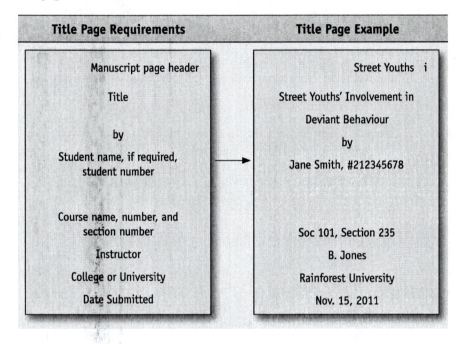

Title Page Requirements	Title Page Example
Manuscript page header	Street Youths i
Title	Street Youths' Involvement in Deviant Behaviour
by	by
Student name, if required, student number	Jane Smith, #212345678
Course name, number, and section number	Soc 101, Section 235
Instructor	B. Jones
College or University	Rainforest University
Date Submitted	Nov. 15, 2011

As a general rule, do not colour, underline, paste, or draw anything on the title page unless directed by your instructor. As well, you should put the title at the top of the page where the text of your term paper starts. Your title should be centred and, if it is longer than one line, double-spaced. The text of your term paper would begin on page three (after the title page and abstract page). With no manuscript page header on the title page and no abstract, the title for your term paper would be repeated where the text starts—on page 1.

5.5.1 Use a Manuscript Page Header (APA Style) if Required by Instructor

If your instructor requires that you include a manuscript page header (APA style), then you must do so. The APA style is to include a manuscript page header on *every page* of your term paper, including your title page, abstract, and references page. The manuscript page header includes the following:

- One to three significant words from your title
- The page number

This header is placed in the top right corner of your title page (see the title page example). For example, your term paper would have the following *manuscript page header* for a term paper that is entitled "Street Youths' Involvement in Deviant Behaviour" and that uses the third way of numbering pages (from the Introduction):

- The *title page,* as page one, would be as follows:

  Street Youths   i

  (Note that there are five spaces between the text and the page number.)

- The *abstract page,* as page two, would be as follows:

  Street Youths   ii

- The page where *the text of your term paper starts*, page three, would be as follows:

  Street Youths   1

Note that if your instru*ctor does not require you to have* a manuscript page header, then the title page would be the same *except* there would be no manuscript page header and no page number on the title page.

An instructor who does not require a manuscript page header may also not require an abstract. In this case, page number 1 would be in the top right-hand corner and would start where the text of your term paper begins.

5.6 What Do I Need to Do to Produce My Final Copy?

If you have just written a five-argument term paper, check to see how many words or pages the paper is (omit the title, abstract, and references page). For now, it is worthwhile to remember the word or page count for your second term paper.

Before you submit or hand in your term paper, you should do the following:

- Check it over one final time to make sure it is error-free and complete.
- Make a full backup copy of your completed term paper in your separate storage device.
- Print two copies: one for your instructor and one for you.
- Make sure you do not attach any material unless directed by your instructor.
- Staple the top left-hand corner: make sure that the pages are in order.

Then, hand it in on the due date, at the start of your class.

As you progress in your studies, you will gain more control over writing your term paper so that it will increasingly reflect your personal argumentative style within the social science research community. With the basic knowledge that you have gained here, you can continue to improve and expand your social science term papers.

Chapter Summary

Write a term paper draft:

- Use required writing skills—spelling, grammar, punctuation, quotations, appropriate language.
- Write your draft—use sentences, paragraphs, and transitions.
- Follow this general format and process:
  Introduction to aim, transition to aim sentence, aim sentence
  Transition from aim to definition of concepts, define concepts in aim
  Transition from definitions to organization of arguments, organize arguments
  Transition from organizing arguments to presenting arguments, then the arguments, presenting the point of an argument, transition from point to evidence, and presentation of the evidence in support of your point
  Transition from one argument to another argument
  Transition from argument to conclusion, conclusion
  References
- Consult your instructor about your draft.

Revise your draft:

- Proofread draft and correct basic writing errors, ensure a coherent, unified paper.

Format your term paper:

- Follow APA style rules for appearance from title page to references page.
- Write abstract (if required).
- Follow APA style format for abstract.
- Include importance of aim, aim sentence, and arguments as conclusions to aim.

Create a title page:

- Follow APA style—include a manuscript page header (if required).

Produce final copy:

- Check it one final time before making backup copy, printing two copies, and handing it in.

Checklist for Writing Term Paper

Write a term paper draft:

- ☐ Did you make a copy of your outline to create a draft term paper file?
- ☐ Did you make a backup copy of your draft term paper file?
- ☐ Did you write your draft term paper using correct writing skills, proper sentences, paragraphs, and transitions?
- ☐ Did you follow the format and process below in writing your draft?
  Introduction to aim sentence
  Transition to aim sentence
  Aim sentence
  Transition from aim to definitions
  Definition of concepts in aim
  Transition from definitions to organizing arguments
  Organization of arguments
  Transition from organizing arguments to arguments
  Presentation of arguments
  Presenting the point of an argument
  Transition from point to evidence
  Presenting the evidence in support of your point
  Transition from one argument to another argument
  Transition from argument to conclusion
  Conclusion
  References
- ☐ Did you consult with your instructor about your draft term paper?
- ☐ Did you make the revisions as directed by your instructor?

Revise your term paper:

- ☐ Have you set your draft aside for a day or two?
- ☐ Did a more experienced writer check it?
- ☐ Did you proofread it for errors in writing, transitions, and consistency?
- ☐ Is your paper written as a coherent and unified whole?

Format your term paper:

- ☐ Is your entire paper double-spaced, except long quotes over 40 words (which are single-spaced)?
- ☐ Are your references in correct alphabetical sequence and formatted according to APA style?

Write an abstract (if required):

☐ Does your abstract contain the importance of your aim, your aim, and some major arguments as conclusions to your aim?

☐ Is your abstract on a separate page after the title page?

☐ Is your abstract formatted according to APA style requirements (a block of text, no indentation, up to 120 words, double-spaced)?

Create a title page:

☐ Did you create a proper title page by following APA style requirements?

☐ Did you create a manuscript page header—yes or no (if no, first page number starts with text of paper)?

Produce final copy:

☐ Did you make a backup copy of your term paper in a separate storage device before printing?

☐ Did you print two copies—one to hand in to your instructor and the second one to keep?

☐ Did you staple the top left corner of your term paper (without adding anything to it unless directed by instructor)?

☐ Did you hand it in at the start of class?

Recommended Web Sites

The OWL at Purdue University—on academic writing in general:
   http://owl.english.purdue.edu/owl/

The OWL at Purdue University—on transitions and transitional devices:
   http://owl.english.purdue.edu/owl/resource/574/01/

Recommended Readings

On general writing for your term paper:
   Fowler, H.R., Aaron, J.E., & McArthur, M. (2008). *The Little Brown handbook*. Toronto: Pearson/Longman.
   Reinking, J.A., von der Osten, R., Cairns, S.A., & Fleming, R. (2007). *Strategies for successful writing: A rhetoric, research guide, reader, and handbook*. Upper Saddle River, NJ: Pearson.

On revising a term paper:

Booth, W.C., Colomb, G.G., & Williams, J.M. (2008). *The craft of research*. Chicago: University of Chicago Press.

Norton, S., & Green, B. (2006). *Essay essentials*. (4th ed.). Scarborough, ON: Thomson/Nelson.

On writing in psychology:

Dunn, S.D. (2004). *A short guide to writing about psychology*. New York: Pearson.

Northey, M., & Timney, B. (2007). *Making sense: A student's guide to research and writing: Psychology and the life sciences*. (4th ed.). Toronto: Oxford University Press.

Szuchman, L.T. (2008). *Writing with style: APA style made easy*. (4th ed.). Belmont, CA: Thomson Wadsworth.

On writing in sociology:

Giarrusso, R. (2008). (Ed.). *A guide to writing sociology papers: The sociology writing group*. (6th ed.). New York: Worth.

Johnson, Jr., W.A., Rettig, R.P., Scott, G.M., & Garrison, S.M. (2006). *The sociology student writer's manual*. (5th ed.). Upper Saddle River, NJ: Pearson Prentice Hall.

On writing in the social sciences:

Cuba, L. (2002). *A short guide to writing about social science*. New York: Longman.

Roe, S.C., & den Ouden, P.H. (Eds.). (2003). *Designs for disciplines: An introduction to academic writing*. Toronto: Canadian Scholars' Press.

Chapter 6
Writing the First Social Science Book Review

In addition to a term paper, you may be required to write a book review. Writing a review in the social sciences generally means that you will be required to evaluate or critique another author's work. A *critique* means that you must make positive, neutral, and negative evaluations or comments about someone's research and writing. A book review or a critique of an article in the social sciences is thus a critical evaluation of an author's work.

Learning to do a book review or article critique has many benefits, including the following:

- You will learn in some detail about another author's work.
- You will discover how a work has been organized and presented.
- You will be prepared to analyze texts or documents.
- You will gain practice for further reviews.

This chapter will show you how to use the basic social science argumentative format and process to help you start to write a social science book review. You can also apply this to writing a review of an article. You will need to undertake the following to prepare for a review:

- Have a competent, working knowledge of the previous chapters. This is important because some of the material and requirements for writing a social science review are similar to those for writing a term paper.
- Know that a book review requires you to use the basic social science argumentative format and process to evaluate another author's work (and any additional items).
- Read this entire chapter before you start your review. You should recognize some material from previous chapters that is presented here in condensed form to assist you in writing your book review.

This chapter will present the following:

1. The requirements for your book review
2. The book review outline
3. How to write your first social science book review
4. The format of a book review

5. The format of the title page
6. How to submit your final copy
7. Suggestions for writing an article critique

6.1 What Are the Requirements for My Book Review?

As with a term paper, your instructor will inform you of the requirements for your book review.

Reminder
Record and follow your instructor's directions. This is your responsibility.

6.1.1 Know What Kind of Book Review Is Required

There are two general requirements involved in undertaking a book review:

- The first requirement is that it must be a critical review or an evaluation of a book. Your evaluation must make positive or negative comments about an author's work—in other words, you must form an opinion about the work. You do this by reading the book and making comments.
- Your book review will have its own particular requirements. These specific requirements are listed below. Change anything as required by your instructor.

Specific Requirements

Title Page (APA Style)
- Check to see what is required on your title page.
- Check to see if a manuscript page header is required. Most instructors do *not* require this for a book review. This chapter assumes that none is required.

Page Numbers
- First page number starts with the text of the book review.

Title of Book Being Reviewed
- Place title on first page where book review starts.
- Give complete APA style reference.

Book Review Due Date
- You must record when the book review is due to be handed in.

Outline of Book Review
- Most instructors do not require an outline for a book review.
- Use the First Social Science Outline in Appendix C to record your arguments about the work (adjust for more or fewer words, pages, or arguments for length).
- Make any changes to the outline to suit instructor requirements for a book review.

- *Record the due date for outline*, if you are required to hand one in.

Book Review Length
- Book reviews are usually shorter than term papers, so brevity in writing is very important.
- Length is generally stated in minimum to maximum number of words (for example, 1200–1500 words). (Your instructor may also state the minimum and maximum length in page numbers or in number of arguments: 6–8 pages or 5–8 arguments. *Record and follow this requirement.*)
- Book review length is taken *very seriously*, and your instructor may impose *penalties* for violating the minimum and maximum length.

Margins, Font Size, and Type
- You must use one-inch margins, the size of the required font, such as 12 point, and the font type, such as Times New Roman.

References (APA Style)
- You may or may not be asked to use references in your book review.
- Using more references (books and periodicals) will mean a more informative book review.
- Check with your instructor to see if any additional references are required and what kinds are acceptable.

Here is a checklist of the previous requirements.

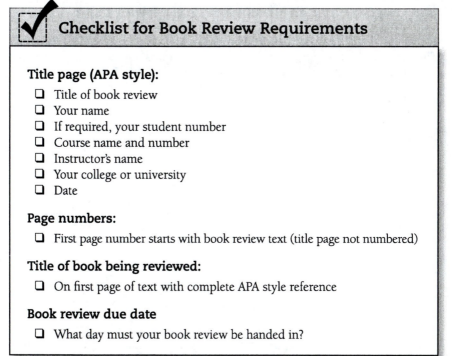

✔ Checklist for Book Review Requirements

Title page (APA style):
- ❏ Title of book review
- ❏ Your name
- ❏ If required, your student number
- ❏ Course name and number
- ❏ Instructor's name
- ❏ Your college or university
- ❏ Date

Page numbers:
- ❏ First page number starts with book review text (title page not numbered)

Title of book being reviewed:
- ❏ On first page of text with complete APA style reference

Book review due date
- ❏ What day must your book review be handed in?

Outline of book review:

- ❑ Use The First Social Science Outline in Appendix C
- ❑ Change outline as directed by your instructor
- ❑ *Due date for outline*, if required to be handed in

Book review length:

- ❑ Number of words
- ❑ Number of pages
- ❑ Number of arguments

Margins, font size, and type:

- ❑ One-inch margins
- ❑ 12-Point font size
- ❑ Times New Roman font type

References (APA style):

- ❑ Minimum number of references
- ❑ Acceptable kinds of references

6.2 How Do I Work on My Book Review Outline?

The basic social science argumentative format and process can be used as a guideline to help you evaluate another author's work. Here are the standard features:

- Aim
- Definition of concepts
- Organization of arguments
- Presentation of arguments
- Conclusion
- In-text citations
- References

Begin your book review outline by doing the following:

- Create a computer file of a complete book review outline (use Appendix C: The First Social Science Outline as a guide).
- Make any other changes to your outline as directed by your instructor.
- Make a backup copy of your outline in a separate storage device (for example, USB flash drive). Regularly make backup copies of your original file.

Your social science book review outline is thus similar to the term paper one. You may, however, have to increase the arguments section to allow for more arguments.

Reminder
You may need to reread Chapter 1 for the meanings of the words in the basic social science argumentative format and the priorities for doing research.

Now, work on the *first-priority* items of the basic social science argumentative format and process for your book review.

6.2.1 Work on First-Priority Items in Outline

Recall the first-priority items in the basic social science argumentative format and process:

- Aim
- Arguments
- In-text citations
- References

Here is how these first-priority items are used for your book review:

- Your opinion of the author's book will become your aim sentence.
- Your opinion will be based on the kinds of arguments that you will make about the work: generally positive, undecided, or negative.
- The in-text citations will be the actual references from the book that you will use to substantiate your points and evidence.
- Any additional references that you use in your book review should also be recorded in your outline.

The *inductive process* for developing your aim or opinion about the work is as follows:

- Start with a working aim or stay neutral about the work being reviewed.
- Develop individual arguments first and then categorize all your arguments as positive, undecided, or negative.
- Create your book review aim inductively based on the general categorization of your arguments.

The first-priority items are now presented in more detail, starting with the aim.

Aim

The aim sentence for your book review will present your opinion about the author's work. You may have formed an early opinion of the book by skimming through it. Treat your opinion as a *working aim* since you have no arguments yet to support your evaluation.

Here are some guidelines about using a working aim for a book review:

- Keep your working aim under control, and remember that it may be revised.
- Do *not* use your working aim to look for arguments to fulfill it because this is unfair to the author—just as it would be unfair to you if someone evaluated your work this way.

- Stay *neutral* at the outset so that you can look at the positive and negative arguments of a work before you create and finalize your aim.

Arguments

An argument for a book review consists of the following:

- The point you wish to make
- The evidence to support the point or missing evidence from the book

Taken together, the point and evidence make an argument. Note the following about arguments:

- Where you are making a point and are unable to find evidence in the book, then this may be a negative argument.
- Record your individual points and evidence about the work in your book review outline.

Follow these guidelines about presenting a point and evidence:

- Do not present more than one point per argument; each point will require evidence or proof from the author's work. Many reviewers in popular magazines present many points without providing evidence for some of them. Your review will be more convincing if you state only one point with supporting evidence.
- In general, present only one clear example for each point. Avoid long, detailed descriptions from the author's work that fail to state an exact point with the evidence provided. Paraphrase or summarize descriptions to a few sentences.

Start your review by *reading* the work in its entirety, preferably twice. You are reading this book in order to

- find and recognize the features of the basic social science argumentative format and process in the book;
- see what other items have been added and used in the book;
- familiarize yourself with and determine the sequence of the book's contents; and
- prepare yourself to make arguments about all of the preceding.

Here is a very general and brief list of some *contents of a book* about which you might create arguments:

- Aim, which may be stated as purpose, focus, or a research question
- Theory or theoretical perspectives
- Definition of the concepts in the purpose of the book, which may refer to theory
- Research methods, which may include various aspects, such as design of research
- Organization of arguments, which will most likely refer to the sequence of the various headings or themes of the book
- Presentation of arguments, usually separated and presented in various parts, such as data, analysis, discussion
- Conclusion

- References (there may be a glossary of terms and an index)

Note that this list, of what an author's book might contain, includes the basic social science argumentative format and process, plus theory and research methods. However, an author might use words that differ from those used in the basic social science argumentative format and process. For example, the aim may be called the purpose or it may be stated as a question to be addressed in the research.

As well, most books will have more content than the basic social science argumentative format and process. A book will generally include theory and research methods. The word *theory* (or *theories*), in the social sciences, means to provide an *explanation* of the arguments, points, or evidence. The various disciplines or fields of study have different theories or theoretical perspectives to explain research. *Research method* (or *methods*) refers to the different kinds of systematic and planned investigations that are carried out to obtain evidence or information about a problem or question. Each discipline or field of studies has acceptable research methods that create the evidence for its arguments and theories. The theory (or theories) of the book are used to explain the evidence (or findings, results) in order to draw conclusions about the book's aim.

In evaluating a book, *make notes*, write comments, or ask questions about its contents. Remember to write each one of your comments separately as a point in your outline, making sure to add the page reference. As a beginning student, make your comments by *following the content sequence of the book*. In other words, your remarks should start where the book starts and end where the book ends. Much thought and planning has gone into organizing a book before it is published, so it makes sense to follow that organization.

By following the sequence of the book's contents you will learn how the book has been coherently and logically organized and the reasons for that organization. In reading the sequence of the book, make notes about points and evidence on the following:

- What you liked or were positive about
- What you were unsure about or questioned
- What you disliked or were negative about

Here are some additional questions to help you make comments about the book for your outline (Northey & Timney, 2007, pp. 48–50):

- Are there any assumptions about each of the characteristics, starting with the author's purpose or aim?
- Does the evidence support the aim? Are there missing parts?
- Would a different research method be helpful?
- Are there additional theories that would explain the evidence or data?
- Do all the parts of the work support each other, or are there gaps?
- Is the book coherent and logical? Are there any problems in following what the author has presented?
- Is the conclusion of the book justified? What future research might be useful?

Some examples of the kinds of positive or negative comments (meaning your points and evidence from the book) that you might make are as follows:

- The author's aim is either clearly expressed or difficult to determine.
- The key concepts are either clearly defined and explained or are assumed.
- The author's work is both well organized and logical, or vague about how some parts relate to each other.
- The arguments may be either very convincing, with reliable and valid evidence, or very general and weak and lacking proof.
- The conclusion may outline solid support for the aim and the arguments, or it may be vague and unclear.
- Add comments on contributions to the relevant theory, as well as on the appropriateness of the author's research methods.

Tips | Check out the questions at the end of this chapter on writing an article critique for more evaluative comments.

Record your points and evidence about any of the preceding in the arguments section of your outline (plus the page reference). Attempt to create as many arguments as possible so that you can omit the weaker ones later. Your arguments should include some or all of the following that would apply to the book:

- The purpose of the book, usually related to a theory or theories
- The research method or methods used
- The evidence (quantitative and/or qualitative data) presented
- The theoretical explanation of the evidence
- The degree to which the purpose was met and any advancements made in concluding the book

Take any of the preceding into account as you complete your outline of the arguments about the book. These arguments are vital for good, quality research. Once you have completed your arguments, *determine the aim* of your book review in the following general way. *Group the arguments* in your outline into one of three categories as follows:

a. The arguments are generally positive about the book.
b. There appears to be a balance of positive and negative arguments.
c. The arguments are generally negative about the book.

In short, the quality and majority of arguments in one category indicate what your aim should be. *It is the actual arguments that you have created that determine the aim of your book review.* For instance:

- If your arguments are favourable about the work, your aim will have a positive view of the author's work. Your favourable arguments about the author's work will support your positive aim.

- Considerable negative arguments will suggest a negative aim.
- If you have a similar number of positive and negative arguments, you are uncertain about a clear direction for an aim.

The wording of your aim will usually include some or all of the main concepts concerning the purpose of the book. The aim for your book review will be worded to say that you are positive, undecided, or negative about the concepts in the purpose of the book. Record the wording of your aim in the outline.

Tips

In wording the aim sentence of your review, avoid merely stating that you liked or disliked the author's work. Such a statement only emphasizes your emotional response to research material, which is not the main objective of a social science review. Instead, state that you agree or disagree with the purpose of the author's work by including the purpose in your aim sentence.

In-Text Citations

The previous section on arguments has already suggested that you include in-text citations. This point is worth repeating. That is, in your outline, include the page number(s) from the author's book for any material (whether summarized, paraphrased, or quoted) that will be used as in-text citations. Knowing the page number will help you find the author's material quickly in case you need to double-check something. You do not need to record the author's last name as part of your in-text citations because it is assumed that the page number refers to that author.

Including in-text citations in the outline will prepare you to write your book review as follows:

- For paraphrasing and summarizing material from the book, you do not need to include the page number(s). However, your writing must indicate which materials are from the author. Recording the in-text page numbers in your outline will help to remind you what belongs to the author and what your ideas are.
- For quoting from the book, you must provide the page number(s) after the quote. Because the in-text page number(s) for your quotes are already in your outline, this will save you time in writing your book review.

As well, be sure to include in-text citations for all other reference sources in your outline, according to APA style.

References

If you do not have any references other than to the work you are reviewing, do some research to find references to other works in the specific area or topic of your review. Read other reviews (positive or negative) as well to improve your critical analysis of another work. For any additional references, record the complete reference in your outline, according to APA style.

Now that you have an aim and arguments to support that aim, you should *consult with your instructor* about your book review outline. Obtaining feedback from your instructor may

- provide insight on your aim and arguments that you had not considered for the book; and
- challenge you to think about or rethink what you were planning to write.

Although three general kinds of reviews that you might write about an author's work have been covered in this chapter, your instructor might require a different type of a review. *Follow your instructor's directions*, which should include some aspects of writing a review covered in this chapter.

In addition, your instructor might encourage you to write a *positive review* of another author's work. You will thereby learn how to do the following:

- Evaluate another author's work based on certain criteria rather than just on your own personal likes or dislikes.
- Recognize the various parts of someone else's work and the language that is used for making evaluative comments on these different aspects of a work.
- Describe the specific contributions that another author makes.

A positive review is, therefore, a good starting point for a beginning student in order to learn some of the basic aspects involved in writing a review.

Your instructor might also point out that the other two kinds of reviews are more difficult to write:

- The *balanced review* is more difficult to write because it requires you to be more familiar with the subject matter and field of studies. You have to be able to present both sides convincingly and then make a recommendation.
- A good, convincing *negative review* will require knowledge of the field of studies that you will probably not yet have. You may not be aware of gaps in theoretical assumptions and omissions of research methods. These comments are not meant to discourage you from writing this type of review. Just understand the challenge of writing such a review as pointed out by your instructor.

Treat these comments about your review as excellent learning opportunities because your instructor has more knowledge about and experience with the subject matter, discipline, or field of studies.

6.2.2 Work on Second-Priority Items in Outline

After consulting with your instructor and making any changes to your review outline, work on the remaining parts. The items involved here are:

- Definition of concepts in the aim
- Organization of arguments
- Conclusion
- References (if any)

Definition of Concepts in the Aim

You do not need to define every word in the aim sentence of your book review. Instead, *define only the key ideas or concepts*. In a book review, the main concepts usually come from the author's work. Therefore, list those concepts in your book review outline.

You may want to present a quotation for the work's main concepts. Be forewarned, however, that you will need to paraphrase any long definitions. Brevity in a book review is considered crucial so anything more than a few words is considered long. You must learn and be able to condense long definitions while remaining true to their original meaning.

Reminder

For your outline, list the concepts and their definitions in the same order as they appear in your aim sentence.

Organization of Arguments

Many book reviews do not have a separate part that highlights how the arguments have been organized. At best, there may be a sentence or two to suggest *the general sequence of arguments* that will be made. This part of the outline is included to help you order the arguments that you will make and thus assist you in the general wording of those arguments:

- For a positive aim, list your positive arguments first, followed by one or two minor negative arguments.
- For a balanced review, separate your positive and negative arguments, starting with the positive ones. However, a better way is for you to alternate the positive and negative arguments so that you make a positive argument, then a negative one, or vice versa. If you do this, make a list of the sequence you will follow.
- For a negative review, list your negative arguments first, then one or two minor positive arguments.

Conclusion

In the conclusion of your outline, restate your aim and summarize the arguments. Book reviews usually state whether or not to recommend the book. Given that there were three general kinds of reviews presented, there are three possible types of recommendations:

- For a positive aim, you will enthusiastically recommend the work.
- For a balanced or neutral aim, you will have a mixed opinion about the work. At best, you can recommend that the reader of the review (your instructor) read the work and decide for her or himself.
- For a negative aim, you will recommend against reading the work.

References (APA Style)

Make sure that you list any additional *references* in your outline that you used or were required to use for your review. List these reference sources alphabetically according to the last name of the author (see Chapter 3).

Once you have completed your outline, it is worthwhile to *consult with your instructor* again to verify any revisions that you were asked to rethink to see if your outline is complete and to see if any further changes might be required.

6.3 How Do I Write My First Social Science Book Review?

Once you have completed your book review outline you should do the following:

- Make a full backup copy of your book review outline on a separate storage device.
- Print two copies of your outline: one for the instructor (if required) and one for you.

You should now proceed to write your review, keeping in mind the following required writing skills.

6.3.1 Use the Required Writing Skills

You must have good basic writing skills to write a clear and understandable book review, including the following:

- Spelling
- Grammar
- Punctuation
- Quoting
- Appropriate language
- Proper sentences, paragraphs, and transitions

Reminder
See the Introduction and Chapter 5 for more details on writing skills.

Here are some more suggestions to help you write your first book review:

- Maintain an *impartial tone* in writing your evaluations. Even though you are making critical comments about a book, your writing style must be neutral.
- Use appropriate *variety* in what you are presenting, especially in your choice of words, phrases, language, and transitions.
- *Clarify* what you are writing about. This means elaborating on what the words or phrases mean that you are using. *Rephrasing* your writing helps to clarify what you are presenting.
- Clarify how you are going to present what you are writing. In other words, tell

the reader, your instructor, what you are going to write about next. Pointing out what you are doing in your writing will help make your book review more *coherent*.

Improving these writing skills will help you create a clearer and more understandable book review.

6.3.2 Write Your Draft

Use your outline to help you write a draft of your book review. You will be writing the draft of your book review *deductively* by following your outline. Once you have written a draft of your book review, revise it to improve it (see also Chapter 5).

This section will present the three types of book review drafts that were mentioned previously in working on your outline.

Reminder
Follow your instructor's required changes to the three general kinds of reviews presented here.

The three types of book reviews are as follows:

- A positive review of a book
- A balanced review of a book
- A negative review of a book

We will present each one of the preceding in turn. Remember to do the following:

- Add transitions to your writing as you switch from one idea, sentence, or paragraph to the next.
- Delete the headings, which are to be used as a guide only.
- Write your book review as a *coherent, unified* whole (and not as unrelated parts).

A Positive Review of a Book

If you have a positive aim or your instructor suggests that a certain book has made a significant contribution to an area of study, your review will probably be positive. In a positive review, most of the arguments will praise the work while a few will point out weaknesses.

Introduction and aim.
Write an interesting, favourable introduction for a positive review, suggesting that the work is important and well researched. You should include an aim sentence stating that your review of the author's work will be positive.

For example:

> This review will show that the author has clearly demonstrated how family dysfunction produces teen runaways.

> That fetal alcohol syndrome can be prevented is convincingly and clearly presented by this author.

Definition of concepts in the aim.

In writing your review, clarify any concepts or terms in your aim, but do not give formal definitions. Explain any concepts or terms that you used in your aim sentence so that there is no doubt about your meaning. You will probably draw on the author's work for clarification of the concepts. You will usually agree with the author's definitions and will paraphrase them. The wording would therefore resemble the author's. Paraphrasing the definitions indicates that you agree with the way the author uses the concepts. Use this understanding of the definitions to reword or clarify your aim in this positive review.

If you are familiar with the work's general field of studies, state the significance of the field. Then, put the author's work in its analytical and theoretical context, showing your instructor that you understand the overall context of the work you are reviewing. You can then mention the positive contributions the work has made to the field of studies.

Organization of arguments.

You can sometimes omit a paragraph outlining the sequence of arguments that your review will follow because published reviews have stricter space limitations than a published paper. Experienced reviewers are able to suggest the sequence of their arguments through their excellent use of language and knowledge of the specific area. However, as a beginning student who has never written a review, you can briefly state in very general terms what your positive arguments will be, followed by some minor problems with the work.

Do not merely list the arguments you will make in your review. Instead, in several sentences, state how your arguments are organized. Also, do not refer to an example or clarify a point. This is not the place to go into detail. Present this information later in your review.

Presentation of arguments.

Write arguments, with points and specific examples, which show that the work is valuable. Your examples might consist of a quote or paraphrased or condensed material from the author's work.

Below are examples of some general arguments for a review. Notice that the arguments here follow the basic social science argumentative format and process with the addition of theory and research methods. The words are highlighted to show you this. Do *not*, however, italicize words like this in your review.

Suggested positive arguments and what information to add:

The author has a clear and concise statement of the *aim* of the work.

Add what the aim or hypothesis of the work is.

The author's aim falls clearly within a *theory's* framework and will certainly advance part of the theoretical framework being studied.

Add specifically what will be revealed from the aim of this study and how the theoretical knowledge of the field in question will be advanced. You might also say that the theory chosen to explain the study is appropriate and understandable. Give an example from the author's work, showing how the theory explains the study's aim.

The concepts of the aim are *defined* clearly and are easy to understand. The definitions are used consistently throughout the work and provide a solid foundation for the work. Some definitions of the concepts may be appropriate extensions of current usage.

Add examples from the work whenever a separate argument is introduced.

The author's *research methods* yield the kind of information that is required for this work.

Present the positive and negative aspects of the author's research methods.

The research methods yield the relevant kind of data that is necessary to support the arguments of the hypothesis or aim.

Add examples from the work to substantiate any arguments.

The author's work is *organized* logically and is coherent. The sequence that the arguments are presented in assists in understanding the work.

Justify presenting the arguments in this order or give a general observation on how the work is organized.

The *arguments* in the work are convincing; the points are clear and understandable.

Add one impressive example from the work by paraphrasing the point or using minimal quotes.

There is solid evidence to substantiate most of the author's points.

Give an example of evidence that clearly supports a point. Put it in your own words by paraphrasing the author.

The *conclusion* reflects how convincing arguments supported the author's aim. The theory convincingly explains and interprets what the aim and arguments mean in the larger theoretical context.

Add an example for each point.

Once you have given positive arguments, present the one or two negative arguments and their minimal detraction from the work. A negative argument might highlight that a certain point is either missing or vague, and then present evidence of this from the reading. (You might suggest that the author could clarify this in a future work.) A negative comment might also suggest that there is a lack of evidence for a particular point from the reading but that this could be corrected with further research. (Note the pattern of following each negative comment with a statement that it does not detract significantly from the author's work.)

Conclusion.

In a paragraph or two, end your review by restating the positive and favourable opinion of the author's work. Include comments to the effect that the author's position is clear, with sound arguments. Do not include any new points or examples. You can also state the significance of this specific work and how it contributed to the field of studies. Consider including an overall recommendation that other readers would greatly benefit from reading this book.

A Balanced Review of a Book

A review that is balanced will present convincing arguments that both praise the work and point out significant problems with it. The aim of the review is to provide a similar number of positive and negative arguments. A good balanced review will require you to be more familiar with the work, its theory, its research, and the subject area.

There are variations in writing a balanced review. One way is to begin your review by being undecided or neutral in the introduction and aim, presenting balanced positive and negative arguments, and concluding by favouring one side of the arguments over the other. The arguments in the review thereby justify your decision. The reader of your review can then see how you arrived at the positive or negative opinion.

A less common way to write a balanced review is to start the review again by being undecided or neutral in the introduction and aim, presenting balanced positive and negative arguments about the work, but concluding by remaining neutral or undecided and recommending that readers of the work decide for themselves. The review does not recommend either reading it or not. The neutral conclusion is that the reader should consider reading the work to make up her or his own mind. However, your instructor might require you to take a position, with either a positive or negative recommendation.

Consult with your instructor for direction if you want to conclude by being undecided about the work.

Introduction and aim.

Write an introduction that convincingly expresses your indecision or neutrality about the work. For example, you might mention both the favourable and detrimental aspects of the work, which makes the author's work of limited value. Another way is to state that the work is interesting but that its value is not easily understood. Include an aim sentence in your introduction that states that this will be a neutral or balanced review of another author's work.

Examples:

> This review will demonstrate that the author was unclear in showing that teen runaways stem from working-class families.

> It is doubtful that habitual alcohol abuse has an impact on mortality rates as advanced in this work.

Write your review's aim sentence so it suggests that a balance of positive and negative arguments will be put forward in reviewing the work. If you plan to conclude the review with a positive or negative recommendation of the work, include a sentence to that effect. This sentence might state that after presenting positive and negative arguments, you will then be able to offer a tentative recommendation to either read the work, or not.

The aim sentence then sets the direction and focus for the rest of the review. Its wording reflects how the other parts of the review will be worded to give a neutral or balanced view.

Definition of concepts in the aim.

Your comments about definitions of the concepts in the aim should likewise be neutral or undecided. You might agree with parts of the author's definitions of concepts, and disagree with other parts.

For example, you might say something to the effect that the author's definition of *teen runaways* is adequate, but there is some confusion with the concept of *working class*. You might also indicate that there are some problems with the definitions in the work on habitual alcohol abuse.

Quoting or paraphrasing parts of the definition will indicate that you understand their use. Follow up this understanding by rewording or clarifying the aim of your balanced review to indicate where you agree and disagree with the definitions.

Organization of arguments.

As mentioned, this paragraph is usually omitted. However, in your first review there is no harm in giving a brief overview of your arguments. There are two general ways to organize the arguments of the review:

- Keep the positive and negative arguments separate and state that either all the positive or all the negative arguments will be presented first. (This is the block method, Stewart & Allen, 2005, pp. 107–108.)
- Integrate the positive and negative arguments. That is, follow a positive argument with a negative argument, or vice versa. (This is the point-by-point method, Stewart & Allen, 2005, pp. 109–110.)

Once again, consider providing a brief overview of the order that your arguments will follow. It will demonstrate to your instructor that you have given some thought to the organization of your arguments.

Presentation of arguments.

Present both the arguments that are in support of the work and those that are negative about the work. Integrate them, with a negative argument following a positive one. For favourable arguments, include a specific example from the work, using short quotes, paraphrases, and condensed material. For negative arguments, indicate where crucial points and evidence in the work are either lacking or are not addressed.

Below are brief examples and suggestions for neutral arguments used in each of the basic argumentative format and process items. The same recommendations apply here as in the positive review.

Suggested balanced arguments and what information to add:

The author's *aim* is neither clear nor easy to understand.

Add what the purpose of the work is and what is not clear about it.

It is unclear how the author's aim falls within the general *theoretical* framework of the field of studies and it is doubtful that the aim will contribute to that framework.

Add specifically what both supports and detracts from the aim of the work, and how it is unclear that the field of studies will benefit from this work. You might also say that the theory chosen to explain the study is not appropriate or clear. Give an example from the author's work that shows how the theory fails to explain the aim of the study.

There are problems with the way the author *defined* the concepts of the aim.

Provide clear examples of problems with any definitions.

The author's *research methods* yield only partially useful information in the work. Other research strategies would have yielded more relevant data for the arguments and aim.

Provide examples from the work to substantiate any problems with it.

There are problems with the way the work is *organized*. Parts of the work are well organized while others do not flow smoothly.

Provide an example of how the author's work lacks coherence.

Some of the *arguments* are convincing whereas others are incomplete and difficult to follow. Some points are clear and easy to understand while others are confusing.

Provide examples by quoting or paraphrasing from the work.

Some of the points have evidence to support them while others do not have any evidence or data to substantiate them.

Present evidence of this by paraphrasing and condensing material from the work.

The *conclusion* does not clearly show that all the arguments convincingly support the author's aim. The author makes a number of assumptions to show how the arguments relate to the aim of the work. The theory the author used to interpret the aim and arguments is questionable.

Give an example for each point you make.

Conclusion.

In a paragraph or two, restate the aim of your balanced review, highlighting both the favourable and negative arguments about the author's work. Include any possible statements about the strengths and the weaknesses of the work, and its relation to the field of studies.

End your review with a possible recommendation to the effect that after having presented both the positive and negative arguments about the work, you would either recommend or not recommend reading this work. Provide a reason for your decision:

- Some possible reasons for recommending the work include that the favourable arguments arouse more curiosity about the field of studies. The work is worth reading because it gives some valuable insights for future research.
- Recommendations against reading this work might include that there are too many problems with the work to recommend it. Another possible way of wording this might be that the difficulties with the work significantly detract from it.

If you remain neutral (with your instructor's approval), you might make no recommendation either way but might instead urge the reader to use her or his own judgment. You might recommend reading the book, letting readers draw their own conclusions about the work. However, *consult with your instructor before reaching this conclusion.*

A Negative Review of a Book

In a negative review, a majority of the arguments will find the work seriously flawed while a minority, usually just one or two, will mention some positive contributions. A well-written negative review of a work assumes considerable familiarity with the subject and with related theory and research.

Introduction and aim.

Write an introduction stating that there are significant problems with the work that detract considerably from its potential importance. Include an aim sentence stating that this will be a negative review of another author's work.

Examples:

> This review will show that this work does not demonstrate convincingly that working-class teenagers have a higher rate of running away from home than middle- or upper-class adolescents have.

> The author has not shown a relationship between increased advertising of alcohol in the media and an increased rate of alcoholism.

Definition of concepts in the aim.

If your review has a negative aim, there are probably significant problems with the definitions of the main concepts. Indicate how you disagree with the definitions of the concepts in the author's work. Your disagreement might be over deviations from generally accepted definitions of concepts in the field, or invalid or contradictory assumptions, or over serious omissions of part or all of the definitions from current research.

You will have to give an example for each point made here. Your examples will come from both the author's work (omissions, assumptions, or contradictions) and from the works of other authors in the field (what those authors include in their works, and their reasons and logic for doing so). Your examples will show your instructor that you understand the problems with the definitions and how they relate to the field of studies.

Organization of arguments.

As mentioned with the other kinds of reviews, this paragraph is sometimes omitted for the sake of brevity. However, compose a few sentences anyway if you have never written a social science review. State very briefly the negative arguments that you will present, followed by the minor contributions. This sets the stage for the specific arguments that you will make.

Presentation of arguments.

Write arguments that show that the work is negative. Below are suggestions and examples of arguments worded negatively for the same criteria as the previous reviews. The previous recommendations apply here as well.

Suggested negative arguments and what information to add:

The author does not have a clear and concise *aim*. The aim is convoluted and difficult to understand.

For example, you might add that there are too many concepts to give this work a clear, definite focus.

Another problem is that the aim does not advance anything new and is merely a summary of a selected part of the field.

State what the serious problem(s) is with the aim of the work.

The author's aim or purpose does not fall within the *theoretical* framework of the work. The theoretical framework of the work is difficult to understand. Also, a different theoretical framework is better at explaining or interpreting the author's work.

Add an example for each point, including the different theoretical framework and how it is better at explaining the author's work than the one the author used.

The concepts of the aim are not *defined* clearly. Parts of the definition are missing, misleading, or vaguely worded. The concepts and definitions are used inconsistently or inappropriately. There is no attempt to build on current knowledge or to use definitions as they currently exist in the literature.

Each point means you need to provide a convincing example.

The author's *research methods* used to support the work's focus do not yield the kind of information that is required for this work. There are other research methods, quantitative or qualitative, that would yield more relevant data needed to support the hypothesis's arguments.

Provide examples to substantiate any arguments.

The work is not *organized* coherently. The sequence of arguments is haphazard and makes the work confusing.

Present an example from the work of each problem that you point out.

The majority of *arguments* in the work are not convincing. Most of the points in the work are unclear. These points need considerable elaboration in order to be understood.

Present an example of this from the work.

Many points also have no evidence or data to support them and are only opinions.

As an example, present a point that has no evidence to support it.

Overall, the arguments in the work are weak and seriously flawed.

The *conclusion* of the work does not hold up because of the weak arguments made to support the aim. There is no attempt to show how arguments support the aim of the author's work. The theory does not interpret convincingly what the aim and arguments mean in the larger theoretical context.

Give an example for each point.

Once you have presented the negative arguments, then put your one or two positive arguments forward. Your positive arguments might highlight that a certain point is valid and then you might give evidence from the reading. Another positive comment might be that there is important evidence for a particular point from the reading. Offer these positive comments in the context of the overwhelming negative arguments. The usual opinion will be that these positive comments do not make a significant contribution to the field. In short, the problems with the work outweigh its minor contributions.

Conclusion.

In a paragraph or two, state why the reading was negative and that no significant contribution was made to the field. You will usually conclude that other readers will not benefit from reading the book or article. In short, you cannot recommend the author's work.

6.3.3 Consult Your Instructor

Now that you have a draft of your book review, consult with your instructor one final time. Make sure that you have included your instructor's suggestions from previous consultations.

6.3.4 Revise Your Draft and Submit Your Book Review

Before you revise the draft copy of your book review it is a good idea to do the following:

- Set it aside for a day or two.
- Read your work out loud.
- Find someone with more writing experience and familiarity with the subject to read and check your work before handing it in.

Wondering how your book review might be evaluated? There are at least two general ways—completeness and individual criteria.

Completeness: Do you have all the required parts?	Individual Criteria: How well did you do on each part and on overall coherence?
• Introduction and aim sentence • Definition of concepts • Organization of arguments • Presentation of arguments • Conclusion • In-text citations • References	• Writing skills • Introduction and aim sentence • Definition of concepts • Organization of arguments • Presentation of arguments • Conclusion • In-text citations • References

Note: Your instructor may change, delete, or add to these minimum criteria.

Now proofread your draft. To *proofread* means to read your review again, checking for any errors. When proofreading, you should check for the following:

- Clear use of words and basic writing skills—replace redundant words and use variety for overused words.
- Neutral tone is used in your writing.
- That all required parts are included—there are no missing parts, from introduction to references.
- Coherent and consistent writing—your writing is logical and deals with each idea or thought in its proper sequence.
- Clear and effective arguments—each point and supporting evidence relates to each other and is convincing.
- Unified book review—your writing relates clearly every idea, paragraph, or part of the review.

Remember that virtually all instructors will evaluate basic writing abilities as part of a book review. Proofreading your work is essential. As well, you should make sure that your book review is formatted properly.

6.4 How Do I Format My Book Review?

To *format* your book review refers to its appearance. There are certain APA style rules about the way your book review must look. The following items are general standards for formatting:

- Use standard letter-size paper.
- Use one side of the page only.
- Use one-inch margins.
- Use 12-point font size.
- Use Times New Roman font.

- For references page, centre the word *References* at the top of the page, place all references in correct alphabetical sequence, and indent second and any additional lines a half-inch.
- For quotations over 40 words, single-space as a block of text and indent the entire quote a half-inch with no quotation marks.
- Double-space the rest of the book review, including references.

If your instructor requires any changes to these items, you must follow those directions.

6.5 How Do I Format the Title Page (APA Style)?

The title page is a separate page with all items centred and double-spaced. Your instructor may require the following on your title page:

- The words *Book Review* and the complete title of the book
- Your name (and, if required, your student number)
- The course name, number, and section number
- Your instructor's name
- Name of your college or university
- The due date (the date by which the book review must be submitted)

Here is an example of requirements for a title page, and an example of what your title page should look like:

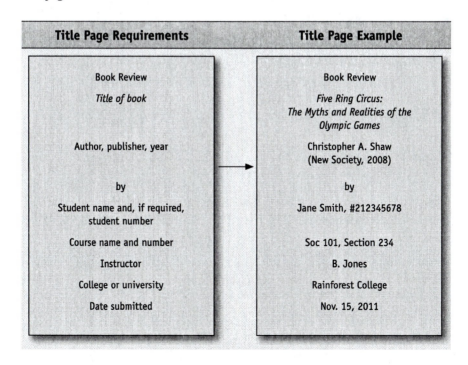

Title Page Requirements	Title Page Example
Book Review	Book Review
Title of book	*Five Ring Circus: The Myths and Realities of the Olympic Games*
Author, publisher, year	Christopher A. Shaw (New Society, 2008)
by	by
Student name and, if required, student number	Jane Smith, #212345678
Course name and number	Soc 101, Section 234
Instructor	B. Jones
College or university	Rainforest College
Date submitted	Nov. 15, 2011

As a general rule, do not colour, underline, paste, or draw anything on the title page unless directed by your instructor. As well, you should do the following:

- Put the full reference of the book at the top of the page where the text of your book review starts.
- Make sure that the text of your book review starts your page numbering with the number 1 only on the right side (as a header with no added text).

6.6 What Do I Need to Do to Produce My Final Copy?

If you have just written a five-argument book review, check to see how many words or pages you used (omit the title and references pages). For now, it is worthwhile to remember the word and page count for your next book review. Before you submit or hand in your book review, you should do the following:

- Check your book review over one final time to make sure it is error-free and complete.
- Make a full backup copy of your completed book review in your separate storage device.
- Print two copies: one for your instructor and one for you.
- Make sure you do not attach any material unless directed by your instructor.
- Staple the top left-hand corner: make sure that the pages are in order.

Then, hand your paper in on the due date, at the start of your class.

6.7 How Do I Write an Article Critique?

You can use the previous material on writing a book review to write a review of an article, which is commonly referred to as an *article critique*. If you have not done so, you should read this entire chapter to get an overview of doing a review. This overview will help you to understand the adaptations and further suggestions based on doing a book review that are presented here.

Reminder

- Adapt the book review outline to *create an article critique outline*.
- Consult with your instructor as you progress through the steps of completing your article critique outline and *revise* it as necessary.
- For your outline and eventual writing, focus on the author(s) and what she or he says. For example, state what the author's aim is and not the article's aim.

Writing an article critique involves summarizing and evaluating what an author has written. Your instructor may require you to summarize and evaluate an article in one of two ways (or possibly a variation of these):

- A separate summary and evaluation of an article
- An integrated summary and evaluation of an article

6.7.1 Write a Separate Summary and Evaluation of an Article

Your instructor may require you to keep the summary and evaluation of an article separate. Your article critique would then start with a summary of an author's work followed by your evaluation or opinion of it.

There are a number of good reasons for you to learn how to summarize or condense an author's work:

- To recognize the various significant parts of an article
- To understand what the author has presented
- To determine the most significant features of an author's work
- To write your understanding of the main arguments of an author's work in a condensed way
- To write your summary in a neutral and unbiased tone or manner

Summarizing an author's work may include the following significant parts or a variation of them (the keywords used in doing a book review are also highlighted here):

- Introduction, background, aim, and important concepts of the author
- Methods and how they were designed to investigate the aim
- Arguments presented based on evidence and analysis of the results
- Conclusions concerning the relation between the aim and the analysis of the findings

Tips | If your instructor does not specify a required format in which to present your summary, then use the general headings or organization of the article as your guide.

Here are some general questions for each of these four parts to help you summarize an author's work:

- In the introduction and background, what is the main consideration (for instance, theoretical or practical) that leads the author to formulate this aim?
- What is the author's aim (which may be worded as a purpose, thesis, hypothesis, problem, or question)?
- What are the main concepts in the author's aim, and how are they defined or clarified?
- Which specific methods and their design does the author use to study the aim?
- What is the author's rationale for using those methods?
- How does the author use those methods?

Reminder
You may need to review your textbooks and lectures to ensure that you understand the methods and their design.

- What is the general evidence (or results or findings) of the study?
- How does the author analyze these results?
- Can you state the most important arguments of the author's analysis as it pertains to the results?

Tips Use the author's conclusion to help you determine the most important arguments.

- What are the author's conclusions between the aim and the analysis of the findings?
- Which parts of the aim were supported by the findings and to what degree?
- How does the author justify the support for the aim of the study?
- How does the author rationalize the findings that did not support the aim?
- Does the conclusion suggest a logical further study?

Knowing how to summarize an author's work competently and fairly helps to prepare you to add your evaluative comments. There are two general kinds of related evaluations that you can add to your summary of an article. They may be referred to as *internal* and *external* evaluations or critiques. Both kinds are usually included in a critique (without specifying which kind is being used). We use them here separately to show you that learning more theories and research, as you progress in your courses and studies, will be a great source for improving your evaluations, especially external critiques. Both kinds of evaluations will also help you understand some of the processes involved in making evaluations.

An *internal critique or evaluation* is concerned primarily with assessments (positive and negative) that focus on the article itself. This kind of evaluation is concerned mainly with arguments for each part of the article and the relationship of each part to the author's overall intended aim. Positive and negative arguments are presented that centre primarily on the article. If you are unfamiliar with the topic or subject matter contained in the author's work, then you may need to consult some reference sources to help you understand it.

Tips For areas or aspects with which you might disagree with an author, consider wording your comment as a *suggested improvement* instead of simply stating your disagreement.

Your answers to the following questions will help you create some positive and negative internal arguments about an author's work:

- Is the author's writing of each part of the article clear and understandable, or are there vague and convoluted parts that can be improved on? Are there any gaps or omissions?
- Does each part relate consistently to the next, or are there some inconsistencies?

- What does the author assume in the article? Is this assumption(s) reasonable or unreasonable?
- Would clarifying some assumptions make the author's work more convincing?
- Is the author's aim developed rationally from the introductory background?
- What would improve it?
- Does the author use concepts in a consistent way throughout the study? Are there any inconsistencies that need to be clarified?
- Is the method(s) clear and reasonable to investigate the aim? Are any shortcomings clarified?
- Are the findings reliable and justified?
- Are the explanations of the results credible and persuasive arguments?
- Did the author convince you that the aim of the study was met successfully, or was it unsuccessful? What is the reason(s) for reaching your concluding opinion?
- What was crucial in convincing you?

In addition to positive and negative internal evaluations, there are also external evaluations to consider. An *external critique or evaluation* refers to positive and negative assessments that are predominantly outside of or peripheral to an author's work. The author's work is thus judged positively or negatively compared to other theories, research methods, research findings, and so on.

Reminder
Throughout these questions you may need to research *additional reference sources* to compare or contrast the author's study.

Here are some general external questions to address in making more evaluations:

- Is the author's introductory background a fair or inadequate summary of other works in developing the aim? (You will need to know these additional works.)
- Compared to other works, is the aim innovative or not very interesting? Who is more interesting and why?
- Does the author's use of important concepts compare favourably or not with other works? Is this justified for the study? How can it be improved compared to other works?
- Are there any other research methods, designs, or strategies that could improve the author's investigation?
- Do the results or findings of the study corroborate other studies? Are the results significantly similar or different? What arguments might account for this?
- How does the author's analysis of the results compare with other theoretical arguments? Are the author's argumentative explanations relevant to other theories or not very meaningful?
- How do the conclusions compare to other studies in the insights provided? Do they advance our understanding? Are the implications of the conclusions worth pursuing?
- Could the conclusions be combined with other studies for useful research?

Most likely, you will *not* need to distinguish between the kinds of evaluations (internal or external) that you make. Use the preceding to help you determine the most important arguments that can be made to evaluate an author's work, and include both kinds. Use reference sources as necessary for both.

6.7.2 Write an Integrated Summary and Evaluation of an Article

An article critique that requires you to integrate a summary and evaluation of that article means that you are expected to express your opinions as you accurately and fairly present an author's work. This general kind of format for an article critique (or possible variation of it) assumes that you are able to summarize an author's study and can make internal and external argumentative evaluations of it (as presented in the previous section).

Gaining experience in writing a separate summary and evaluation will assist you greatly before undertaking a critique that requires you to integrate them. Now, you are expected to present your opinions on the topic of an author's work and to state the author's work fairly. That is, you should present how well or poorly the author's work contributes to the understanding of the general topic or issue. Many reviewers highlight the positive or negative aspects of an author's work as examples of how our knowledge about the subject matter or problem is enhanced or of limited value.

Your opinions are expected to be generally positive or negative arguments. A neutral stance for an article critique is generally not done. *Check with your instructor on what is expected before you start your article critique.*

The process for arriving at an overall opinion of an author's work is presented in the previous book review sections of this chapter. You can change or adapt this process to suit your instructor's requirements for a specific format for your article critique. If your instructor does not specify a format, then consider following the article's headings or organization.

The following questions are offered to you for your consideration in writing this kind of a critique. Answers to these questions combine internal and external evaluations. You should be able to recognize the internal and external focus of these questions from the previous section (you may need to reread this section). These questions are grouped into the same significant parts of an author's work as presented in the separate summary and evaluation section:

- Is the introductory background clearly related to a larger theory or issue? Does the author make similar acceptable or unacceptable assumptions that need to be clarified? What is the most important aspect about the introduction or background concerning the topic or problem?
- Do the introduction and background provide a clear or uncertain rationale for the aim?
- Is the aim presented clearly, or is it difficult to determine? What is the aim? Is the aim innovative or not very original compared to other studies in the field?
- Does the wording of the aim make it easy or somewhat difficult to determine the main concepts and their definition? What are the definitions or clarifications of the main concepts? Are they expressed clearly, or are the meanings vague?

- Are the definitions or clarifications of the main concepts consistent with those of other authors, or do they depart significantly from generally accepted meanings? What are the implications for the current author's methods?
- Are the author's research design and methods appropriate for the aim and concepts of the study? What are they, and are they presented clearly?
- Do the author's research methods correspond favourably with standard practice in the field, or are there some unclear aspects?
- Would the use of other methods significantly improve this study? Is the omission of these acceptable or unacceptable for the author's current purpose?
- What are the results and analysis of these results? Are the results as expected? Are the results reliable and valid? Does the analysis of them present reasonable or unreasonable arguments? Is there anything that might improve them?
- How do these findings and their analysis compare or contrast with similar studies? Do the results corroborate or cast doubt on the arguments of other studies?
- Would an explanation of the results that differs from that of the author's make sense or not?
- Is the conclusion between the aim and the analysis of the results rational, or are there uncertain aspects (and to what degree)?
- What are the main conclusions? Does the author convince you that the stated aim was achieved? What reasons or arguments can you give for being convinced or not?
- How do the conclusions from this author compare to arguments from other studies? Do the conclusions further our understanding of the aim or problem, or not?
- Does the conclusion contribute to and advance our understanding of the subject matter (or problem) in this field, or is this study of limited value?
- Are further logical investigations suggested? Do they appear useful, or would a different direction be appropriate?

You may need to consult references about the topic as well as other works for this integrated summary and evaluation of an article.

The suggestions for undertaking a review that were presented here were meant as a starting point on which to expand your knowledge. As you continue your studies, you will gain more skill in expressing your critical opinion of an author's work within the social science research community.

Chapter Summary

Requirements before you start your book review:

- Record the specific requirements from your instructor in the checklist.

Work on your book review outline:

- Create a book review outline using the First Social Science Outline in Appendix C.
- Start working with the first-priority items of the basic social science argumentative format and process.
- The aim will be your overall opinion of the work; the arguments will be your points and evidence about the work, including theory and research methods (either positive, undecided, or negative).
- Read the contents of the book and make notes about points and evidence that you felt were positive, undecided, or negative.
- Record your points, evidence, and page references from the book in the arguments section of the outline.
- Determine the aim of the book based on your completed arguments (were they mostly positive, undecided, or negative).
- Research for additional references and reviews by other authors and record them in your outline (as in-text citations and in references page, APA style).
- Consider writing a positive review for your first book review in order to learn to evaluate based on criteria and to become familiar with evaluative language.
- Consult with your instructor about the first-priority items of your review outline.
- Continue with the second-priority items of defining the concepts in your aim, organizing your arguments, and drafting a conclusion (record additional references in outline).
- Consult with your instructor about your completed book review outline.

Write your book review draft:

- Writing skills: use correct spelling, grammar, punctuation, quoting, and appropriate language.
- Write your draft using proper sentences, paragraphs, and transitions.
- Three possible kinds of book reviews are positive, balanced, or negative.
- For a positive review, follow the basic social science argumentative format and process:
  In arguments section, add one or two negative arguments to the majority of positive ones.
  State that the negative ones have minimal impact on the overall positive aspect of author's work.
- For a balanced review, follow basic social science argumentative format and process:

ing this review are as follows:

ral in introduction and aim, present positive and nega-
then in conclusion favour one side over other based on
arguments presented.

2. Start by being undecided in introduction and aim, present both sides in arguments, then remain neutral in conclusion.

- For a negative review, follow basic social science argumentative format and process: In arguments section, add one or two positive arguments to the majority of negative ones.
  State that the positive ones have minimal impact on the overall negative aspect of author's work.
- Consult with your instructor about your draft book review outline.

Revise and hand in book review:

- Set it aside for a day or two.
- Have a more experienced writer check it.
- Proofread it for errors in writing and in consistency.
- Double-space entire book review.
- Format references (if required) in correct APA style.

Create title page (APA style):

- Create proper title page as required.

Produce final copy:

- Make backup of book review in separate storage device before printing.
- Print two copies—one for instructor, one for you.
- Staple top left corner—do not add anything to it unless directed by instructor.
- Hand in at start of class.

Suggestions for writing an article critique:

- Read and adapt all the sections in this book review chapter before starting your article critique.
- Two general formats for writing an article critique are a separate summary and evaluation or an integration of the summary and evaluation.
- A separate summary and evaluation format involves presenting a condensed version of an author's work followed by an internal and external critique or evaluation of it.
- An internal critique or evaluation means to make positive and negative assessments, mainly about the article itself (i.e., its clarity, consistency, and coherence).
- An external critique or evaluation refers to making positive and negative assessments mainly outside of or peripheral to the author's work (i.e., compared and contrasted to other theories, methods, and research studies).
- An integrated summary and evaluation format means to present your opinions about an author's work as you accurately present that work.

Checklist for Writing Book Review and Article Critique

Book review
Write book review draft:

- ☐ Did you make a copy of your outline to create a draft book review file?
- ☐ Did you make a backup copy of your draft book review file?
- ☐ Did you write your draft book review using correct writing skills, proper sentences, paragraphs, and transitions?
- ☐ Did you write a positive, balanced, or negative review of a book?
- ☐ Did you follow the format and process below in writing your draft?
  Introduction to aim sentence
  Transition to aim sentence
  Aim sentence of book review
  Transition from aim to definitions
  Definition of the concepts in aim
  Transition from definitions to organization of arguments
  Organization of arguments
  Transition from organization of arguments to presentation of arguments
  Presentation of arguments
  Presenting the point of an argument
  Transition from point to evidence
  Presenting the evidence in support of your point
  Transition from one argument to another argument
  Transition from argument to conclusion
  Conclusion
  References
- ☐ Did you consult with your instructor about your draft book review?
- ☐ Did you make the revisions as directed by your instructor?

Revise book review:

- ☐ Have you set your draft aside for a day or two?
- ☐ Did a more experienced writer check it?
- ☐ Did you proofread it for errors in writing, transitions, and consistency?
- ☐ Is your book review written as a coherent and unified whole?

Format book review:

- ☐ Is your entire book review double-spaced, except long quotes over 40 words (which are single-spaced)?
- ☐ Are your references in correct APA style?

Create title page:

❑ Did you create a proper title page by following APA style?

Produce final copy:

❑ Did you make a backup copy of your book review in a separate storage device before printing?

❑ Did you print two copies—one to hand in to your instructor and the second one to keep?

❑ Did you staple the top left corner of your book review (without adding anything to it unless directed by instructor)?

❑ Did you hand your book review in at the start of class?

Article critique

Write article critique:

❑ Did you read, understand, and adapt all sections involved in doing a book review before undertaking an article critique?

❑ For the separate summary and evaluation format of an article critique, did you write a fair summary of the author's work?

❑ Did you include internal and external evaluations of the author's work, suggesting how it might be improved?

❑ For an integrated summary and evaluation format, did you make internal and external evaluations as you accurately presented the author's work?

❑ Did you follow the book review process in completing your article critique, starting with "Revise book review"?

Recommended Web Sites

The library at the University of Wisconsin at Madison—a site that provides links to book reviews in the humanities and social sciences:
    http://researchguides.library.wisc.edu/bookreviews/

The library of Queen's University—a site that provides links to book reviews in the social sciences:
    http://library.queensu.ca/research/guide/book-reviews/social-sciences/

The OWLL (Online Writing and Learning Link) of Massey University (NZ)—on article critiques:
    http://owll.massey.ac.nz/assignment-types/article-critiques.htm

Recommended Readings

On reviewing books and articles

Giarrusso, R. (2008). (Ed.). *A guide to writing sociology papers: The sociology writing group.* (6th ed.). New York: Worth.

Johnson, Jr., W.A., Rettig, R.P., Scott, G.M., & Garrison, S.M. (2006). *The sociology student writer's manual.* (5th ed.). Upper Saddle River, NJ: Pearson Prentice Hall.

Northey, M., & Timney, B. (2007). *Making sense: A student's guide to research and writing: Psychology and the life sciences.* (4th ed.). Toronto: Oxford University Press.

Appendix A

From "What Do I Need to Know About Reading and Writing, and What Skills Do I Need?" in Introduction: Answers to Questions

Spelling

1. The parents hid *their* alcohol from *their* kids.
2. *Their* teen did not *know* to phone home.

Grammar

3. A teen ran away from *home*.
4. Many teens ran away from their *homes*.
5. The family *are* worried about their runaway teen. (*Family* refers to members of a group acting individually and requires a plural verb.)
6. The family *is* worried about its runaway teen. (*Family* is referred to as a whole group and requires a singular verb.)
7. She does not like her parents going out drinking, partying, and staying out late. (This is one way to clear up the confusion of the pronoun *them* to refer to parents and not to *partying, drinking,* and *staying out late*.)
8. She was lying, cheating, and stealing to survive. (*Lying, cheating,* and *had to steal* were not parallel.)

Punctuation

9. A runaway teen may require food, shelter, and clothing.
10. The detox worker stated the policy clearly: "You must follow the rules of this clinic or you will not be allowed to stay."

Sentences

11. The family of the runaway teen is looking for her.
12. She ran away from home. She did not know where she would live or what she would be doing.

Appendix B
A Brief Grammar Reference

Parts of Speech

Every word in a sentence can be categorized as one of eight parts of speech depending on its function in that sentence. The eight parts of speech are as follows: nouns, pronouns, verbs, adjectives, adverbs, prepositions, conjunctions, and interjections.

Nouns

Nouns are words that name people (*Anichka, doctor*), animals (*Buster, dog*), places (*Kuala Lumpur, home*), and things—both concrete things, such as objects or substances (*hospitals, air*), and abstract things, such as qualities or concepts (*sorrow, intelligence*), measures (*metres, years*), and actions (*reading, writing*). In sentences, nouns act as subjects and objects.

Nouns may be classed as proper (beginning with a capital letter) or common (beginning with a lower-case letter). Proper nouns start with capital letters because they name specific people, places, and things (*Dorothy Smith, Moose Factory, Mount Sinai Hospital*). All other nouns are common nouns and begin with lower-case letters (*spatula, school, service*). Nouns may also be classified as countable (a hundred *excuses*) or non-countable (interminable *ennui*).

A noun that refers to a group rather than an individual (*team, company, herd*) is called a collective noun. Nouns made up of two or more words (*Parliament Buildings, father-in-law*) are called compound nouns. The words of a compound noun can be joined (*lighthouse*), separate (*light switch*), or hyphenated (*light-of-my-life*). Compound nouns change over time, often evolving from two words to a hyphenated word to a single word without hyphens. When in doubt about the correct form, consult an appropriate style guide or dictionary.

Pronouns

Pronouns substitute for nouns and allow us to avoid awkward repetition. The word a pronoun substitutes for or refers to is called its antecedent. In the sentence *Nikos forgot his keys*, the pronoun *his* refers to the proper noun *Nikos*, the antecedent.

There are six main types of pronoun: *personal, relative, demonstrative, indefinite, interrogative,* and *reflexive.*

Personal Pronouns

There are six forms of personal pronoun, as shown in the following chart.

	Singular	**Plural**
First person (person/s speaking)	I	we
Second person (person/s spoken to)	you	you
Third person (person/s spoken about)	she, he, it	they

First person refers to the person or people speaking (singular *I,* or plural *we*). *Second person* refers to the person or people spoken to (*you* for both singular and plural); and *third person* refers to the person or people or thing(s) spoken about (singular *she, he, it,* and plural *they*).

Relative Pronouns

Relative pronouns are used to link less important ideas to the main idea of a sentence. They include *that, which,* and *who* (also *whom* and *whose*). The relative pronoun thus performs two jobs at once: it joins a less important (or subordinate) clause to a main clause, and it refers back to its antecedent, the noun it substitutes for. The following examples show the relative pronoun underlined and the antecedent of the pronoun in italics:

Here's the *book* that I promised you.

She took the *train,* which was late.

I had a *TA* who writes science fiction.

Demonstrative Pronouns

Demonstrative pronouns point out or indicate specific things. There are only four demonstrative pronouns: *this* and its plural form, *these*; and *that* and its plural form, *those.*

Indefinite Pronouns

Indefinite pronouns are numerous; like all pronouns, they refer to people, animals, places, and things but not to specific or particular ones. The following are some commonly used indefinite pronouns:

all	any	anybody	anyone	anything
both	each	either	enough	everybody
everyone	everything	few	less	many
more	most	much	neither	nobody
none	no one	nothing	one(s)	other(s)
several	some	somebody	someone	something

Interrogative Pronouns

Interrogative pronouns, such as *what, why,* and *how,* are easy to recognize because they ask questions. The interrogative pronouns in the following examples are in italics.

> *What* would you like to do?
>
> *Which* do you prefer?
>
> *Who* was on the phone?
>
> *Whom* did you invite?
>
> *Whose* are these?

Reflexive Pronouns

Reflexive pronouns refer back to the subject and are also easy to recognize, because they always end in *-self* or *-selves* (*myself, yourself, himself, herself, itself, ourselves, yourselves, themselves*). Reflexive pronouns are used when the subject and object of a verb are one and the same, as in this sentence:

> She cut herself.

Reflexive pronouns are also used for emphasis (sometimes called intensive pronouns):

> I myself collected the data.

Verbs

The verb asserts something, expressing action or a state of being. It is the single most important part of speech since every sentence must have at least one verb, telling what the subject—the person, animal, place, or thing that the sentence is about—is doing, having, or being.

There are two main kinds of verbs: action verbs and linking verbs. Most verbs are action verbs: they express actions (although not necessarily physical ones, for example, *to think* is a kind of action verb). Linking verbs express something about the subject, either identifying the subject (*she is the singer*) or describing the subject (*she is talented*). The most common linking verb is the verb *to be* (in all forms: *I am, you are, she/he/it is, we are, you are, they are, I was, you were,* etc.). Other linking verbs include *appear, become, feel, grow, keep, look, prove, remain, seem, smell, sound, stand, stay, taste,* and *turn.* Most of these can be used as either action or linking verbs, as in the following examples:

> Tamara appeared [*action verb*] in the doorway.

> Tamara appeared [*linking verb*] upset.

The verb in a sentence may consist of a single word (*she sings*), but it may also consist of more than one word (*six months have passed, a week will have passed*). When the sentence verb is a phrase instead of a single word, then the last word—the one that indicates what is happening—is the main (or principal) verb; all the preceding words are auxiliary (or helping) verbs. For example, if I write *I go*, I have a verb made up of a single word, *go*. If I write *I have gone*, I have a verb phrase made up of the auxiliary verb *have* and the principal verb *gone*. The rule holds regardless of the number of auxiliaries. In the verb phrase *must have been leaving*, the principal verb is *leaving*, and all the other words (*must, have,* and *been*) are auxiliaries.

In addition to the verbs *be, have,* and *will,* which are used routinely to form certain tenses (*I am going, I have gone, I will go*), the following verbs are commonly used. They are called modal auxiliaries: *do, must, ought, let, used, need, shall,* and *should; will* and *would; can* and *could;* and *may* and *might.*

Tense refers to the time of a verb's action. Each tense—past, present, and future—has simple, perfect, progressive, and perfect-progressive forms. These convey a range of time relations, from the simple to the complex.

Tense	For actions . . .	Examples
Present	Happening now, occurring habitually, or true anytime	I walk; she walks
Past	Completed in the past	I walked; she walked
Future	That will occur	I will walk; she will walk
Present Progressive	Already in progress, happening now, or still happening	I am walking
Past Progressive	In progress at a specific point in the past or that lasted for a period in the past	I was walking
Future Progressive	Of duration in future, or occurring over a period at specific point in future	I will be walking
Present Perfect	Begun in past and continuing in present, or occurring sometime in past	I have walked
Past Perfect	Completed before others in the past	I had walked
Future Perfect	Completed before others in future	I will have walked
Present Perfect progressive	In progress recently, or of duration starting in past and continuing in present	I have been walking
Past Perfect progressive	Of duration completed before others in past	I had been walking
Future Perfect progressive	Underway for period of time before others in future	I will have been walking

Adjectives

An adjective describes or modifies a noun or pronoun (*a witty remark, a good one*), adding more information to make the meaning of the noun or pronoun more vivid, clear, or precise. The adjective can add information (*a red hat, a large house, a beautiful picture*), or it can limit the meaning to show which, whose, or how many (*this hat, Morgan's book, five pictures*). The words *the* and *a* or *an*—the definite and indefinite articles, respectively—are special kinds of adjectives. They belong in a category of words called determiners: words that show a noun will follow (*a house, an orange, the books*). (Other kinds of adjectives—possessive adjectives, for example—also act as determiners.) A determiner is a kind of marker (specifically, a noun marker). There are other kinds of markers: for instance, auxiliary verbs are verb markers, and adverbs are markers for adjectives and other adverbs. Finally, most adjectives can be compared, as in the following examples: *bright, brighter, brightest; dazzling, more dazzling, most dazzling.*

> Her *radiant* eyes made my heart melt.

[*Radiant* is an adjective that modifies or describes the noun *eyes*.]

> He was *thin* and *pale.*

[*Thin* and *pale* are adjectives modifying the pronoun *he.*]

> *One large brick* house stood on the hill.

[The adjectives *one, large,* and *brick* modify the noun *house.*]

Possessive words can function as nouns (*that bag is Zoe's*), pronouns (*this one is hers*), or adjectives (*Zoe's bag, her bag*). When possessives are used as adjectives, telling to whom or to what something belongs, they are called possessive adjectives. Notice that possessive nouns (*that is Dario's, this is the boy's*) do not change form when they are used as adjectives (*Dario's scarf, the boy's mitten*), but most possessive pronouns do: *the money is mine,* but *that's my money,* and so on (*yours/your, hers/her, ours/our, theirs/their*). In the following example, the possessive adjective *your* in the first part of the sentence and the possessive pronoun *yours* in the second part illustrate the difference:

> *Your* jacket is on the couch; *yours* is in the closet.

In the first part, *your* is an adjective because it has a noun to modify (*jacket*); in the second part, *yours* is a pronoun because it takes the place of a noun.

Adverbs

An adverb can describe a verb, an adjective, or another adverb; it can also describe a whole sentence or clause. When an adverb describes a verb, it shows when (time), where (place), or how (manner) something is done. When it describes an adjective or another adverb, it illustrates the extent or degree of some quality or condition. As noted above, when a verb is stated in the negative, the *not* is an adverb.

> The dancer moves *gracefully.*

[*Gracefully* is an adverb modifying the verb *moves*; it shows manner, how the dancer moved.]

He has a *highly* intelligent daughter.

[*Highly* is an adverb modifying the adjective *intelligent*; it shows the degree to which the man's daughter is intelligent.]

We studied *too* hard.

[*Too* is an adverb modifying another adverb, *hard*.]

Strangely, the auditorium was empty.

[*Strangely* is an adverb that modifies or describes the whole clause, *the auditorium was empty*.]

Prepositions

A preposition is used to introduce a phrase (a group of words without a subject-and-verb combination). The main noun or pronoun in the phrase is called the object of the preposition. Here are examples of such phrases, with the prepositions in italics and the objects underlined:

up <u>the escalator</u>

down <u>the road</u>

into <u>the oven</u>

before <u>the game</u>

Prepositions don't *modify* words the way that adjectives and adverbs do, but in linking the words of the phrase to the rest of a sentence, prepositions show important relationships. For example, notice how the meaning varies when different prepositions are used with the same object:

on the desk

beside the desk

beneath the desk

to the desk

Recall that the noun or pronoun following a preposition is called the object. A prepositional phrase consists of a preposition and its object, often with an article (*the, a, an*) between them. (The definite and indefinite articles are considered adjectives because they always modify nouns or pronouns.) The phrase may also contain modifiers (*on the* <u>comfortable</u> *chair*). The whole structure—the preposition (*on*), the article (*the*), any modifiers of the object (*comfortable*), and the object noun or pronoun itself (*chair*)—is a prepositional phrase.

Additional words between the preposition and its object do not change the grammatical relationship: the preposition and its object form the backbone of the prepositional phrase.

Example:

The house *in the once-green valley* was destroyed *by a raging fire.*

In the first phrase, *in* is the preposition, and *valley* is the object of the preposition; *the* is the definite article, and *once-green* is an adjective modifying the noun *valley*. In the second phrase, *by* is the preposition, *fire* is the object of the preposition, *a* is the indefinite article, and *raging* is an adjective modifying the noun *fire*. The whole prepositional phrase includes the preposition, its object, and any modifiers.

Compound prepositions typically consist of two words, and sometimes three. The following are common examples:

ahead of	apart from	as for	aside from	away from
because of	belonging to	contrary to	due to	inside of
instead of	out of	owing to	rather than	together with
up at	up on	up to	in spite of	for the sake of
on account of	with reference to	with regard to		

A particle is a special kind of preposition that functions as part of a verb, forming something called a verb-particle composite.

Here are two examples:

> He *looked up* the unfamiliar word in the dictionary.

> She *ran into* an old friend.

Notice that the verb in verb-particle composites has a different meaning from that of the verb by itself: people who "look up" words in a dictionary are not looking over their heads, and "running into" old friends is not the same as colliding with them.

Conjunctions

Conjunctions connect words or groups of words in a sentence. Coordinating conjunctions (such as *and, yet, but, for, nor, or, either, neither, yet*) join elements of equal rank in a sentence (single words to single words, phrases to phrases, and clauses to clauses). Subordinating conjunctions (such as *if, since, because, that, while, unless, although*) join subordinate clauses to independent ones.

Conjunctions are indispensable, but they are often misused or treated carelessly. They help to express the logical connections between ideas, so care must be taken to use the right one. The choice of conjunction can radically change the meaning of a sentence:

> *Because* she loved him, she had to leave.

> *Although* she loved him, she had to leave.

Coordinating Conjunctions

The following examples illustrate coordinate elements, with the conjunctions in italics:

> I enjoy apples *and* blueberries.

> She looked in the closet *and* under the bed.

> No one else was at home, *and* I answered the phone.

The first conjunction joins two nouns (*apples, blueberries*); the second joins two phrases (*in the closet; under the bed*); the third joins two independent clauses (*No one else was at home; I answered the phone*).

Subordinating Conjunctions

Subordinating conjunctions are used to show that one idea, expressed in the subordinate clause, leans on another idea, expressed in the independent clause. The following example illustrates this:

I answered the phone *because* no one else would.

Because no one else would is a subordinate clause. Unlike the independent clause, *I answered the phone*, it does not make sense by itself; it needs to be joined to the independent clause to form a complete thought. *Because* is the subordinating conjunction that does the job.

Correlative Conjunctions

Correlative conjunctions come in pairs (*both* . . . *and*; *neither* . . . *nor*; *either* . . . *or*; *not only* . . . *but also*), with each half of the pair introducing one of the two things being joined:

I love listening to music, *both* live *and* recorded.

I enjoy *neither* cooking *nor* cleaning the house.

I want *not only* to live well *but also* to act honourably.

Conjunctive Adverbs

A conjunctive adverb is an adverb that also performs the work of a conjunction, joining sentence elements. It can be used to join two independent clauses. Words used as conjunctive adverbs include the following:

| also | anyhow | besides | consequently | furthermore |
| however | indeed | moreover | nevertheless | thus |

Interjections

Interjections are used to express strong emotion and have no grammatical relation to the rest of the sentence. Some words are always used as interjections (*Hey! Wow! Ouch!*). Words that are generally used as other parts of speech may also be used as interjections (*Great! Oh, no! Too bad!*).

Punctuation

Punctuation is used to separate strings of words into manageable groups and help clarify their meaning. The marks most commonly used to divide a piece of prose or other writing are the period, the semicolon, and the comma, with the strength of the dividing or separating role diminishing from the period to the comma. The period marks the main division into sentences; the semicolon joins sentences (as in this sentence); and the comma (which is the most flexible in use and causes the most problems) separates smaller elements with the least loss of continuity. Parentheses and dashes also serve as separators—often more strikingly than commas, as in this sentence.

Period

A period is used to mark the end of a sentence that is not a question or exclamation. In prose, a sentence marked by a period normally represents an independent or distinct statement; more closely connected or complementary statements are joined by a semicolon (as here).

Periods are used to mark abbreviations (*Wed., Gen., p.m.*). They are often omitted from abbreviations that consist entirely of capital letters (*CBC, EDT, RRSP*) and from acronyms that are pronounced as words rather than sequences of letters (*Intelsat*). They are not used in abbreviations for SI units (*Hz, kg, cm*).

If an abbreviation with a period comes at the end of a sentence, another period is not added:

> They have a collection of many animals, including dogs, cats, tortoises, snakes, etc.

But note:

> They have a collection of many animals (dogs, cats, tortoises, snakes, etc.).

A period is used as a decimal point (*10.5%, $1.65*) and to separate the domains of an e-mail or Web address (*http://www.oupcanada.com*). It is commonly used in British practice to divide hours and minutes in expressions of time (*6.15 p.m.*), where a colon is standard in North American use.

Semicolon

The main role of the semicolon is to join sentences that are closely related or that parallel each other in some way, as in the following:

> Many new houses are being built north of the city; areas to the south are still largely industrial.

> To err is human; to forgive, divine.

It is often used as a stronger division in a sentence that already includes several commas:

> Joanne and Emily went out for dinner, as they usually did on Wednesday; but when, upon arriving at the restaurant, they were told they would have to wait for a table, they went home and ordered Chinese.

It is used in a similar way in lists of names or other items to indicate a stronger division:

> I would like to thank the managing director, Jennifer Dunbar; my secretary, Raymond Martin; and my assistant, David Singh.

Comma

Appropriate use of the comma is difficult to describe as there is considerable variation in practice. Essentially, it is used to give structure to sentences, especially longer ones, in order to make their meaning clear. Too many commas can be distracting; too few can make a piece of writing difficult to read or, worse, difficult to understand.

A comma, typically followed by a conjunction (such as *and, but, yet*), is used to separate the main clauses of a sentence:

> Mario cooked a roast, and Jan baked a pie for dessert.

A comma is not used when the subject of the first clause is understood to be the subject of the second clause:

> Mario cooked a roast and baked a pie for dessert.

It is considered incorrect to join the clauses of a compound sentence with only a comma and without a conjunction:

> ✗ I like skating very much, I go to the local rink every day after school.
>
> ✓ I like skating very much, <u>so</u> I go to the local rink every day after school.
>
> ✓ I like skating very much; I go to the local rink every day after school.

It is also considered incorrect to separate a subject from its verb with a comma:

> ✗ Those with the smallest incomes and no other means, should get more support.
>
> ✓ Those with the smallest incomes and no other means should get more support.

Commas are usually inserted between adjectives preceding a noun:

> An enterprising, ambitious person.
>
> A cold, damp, poorly heated room.

However, the comma is omitted when the last adjective has a closer relation to the noun than the others:

> A distinguished foreign politician.
>
> A lush tropical forest.

An important role of the comma is to prevent ambiguity. Imagine how the following sentences might be interpreted without the comma:

> With the police pursuing, the people shouted loudly.
>
> She did not want to leave, from a feeling of loyalty.
>
> In the valley below, the houses appeared very small.

Commas are used in pairs to separate elements in a sentence that are not part of the main statement:

> I would like to thank you all, friends and colleagues, for coming today.
>
> There is no truth, as far as I can see, to this rumour.
>
> It appears, however, that we were wrong.

A comma is used to separate a relative clause from a noun when the clause is used to provide additional information about the noun but is not essential in identifying it:

> The picture, which hangs above the fireplace, was a present.

In this sentence, the information in the *which* clause (a non-restrictive clause) is incidental to the main statement. Without the commas, it would become a defining or restrictive clause, forming an essential part of the statement by identifying which picture is being referred to:

> The picture that hangs above the fireplace was a present.

Note that a restrictive clause is typically introduced by *that* rather than *which*. Commas are also used to separate items in a list or sequence:

> Emma, Sheilah, and Dorcas went out for lunch.

> The doctor told me to go home, get some rest, and drink plenty of fluids.

It is acceptable to omit the final comma before *and*; however, the final comma has the advantage of clarifying the grouping if a composite name occurs at the end of the list:

> I buy my art supplies at Midoco, Loomis and Toles, and Grand and Toy.

A comma is often used in numbers of four or more digits to separate each group of three consecutive digits starting from the right (e.g., *10,135,793*). In metric practice, a space is used instead of a comma to separate each group of three consecutive figures (*10 135 793*).

A comma is used to introduce a quotation of a complete sentence:

> Nadia exclaimed, "Isn't he fabulous!"

It also substitutes for a period at the end of a quotation if this is followed by a continuation of the sentence:

> "I've never seen such a remarkable athlete," said Stefan.

Colon

The main role of the colon is to separate main clauses when there is a step forward from the first to the second, especially from introduction to main point, from general statement to example, from cause to effect, and from premise to conclusion:

> There is something I forgot to tell you: your mother called earlier.

> It was not easy: to begin with, we had to raise the necessary capital.

It also introduces a list of items:

> This recipe requires the following: semi-sweet chocolate, cream, egg whites, and sugar.

A colon is used to introduce, more formally and emphatically than a comma would, speech or quoted material:

> I told them just last week: "Do not, under any circumstances, open this box."

It is used to divide hours and minutes in displaying time (*6:30 p.m., 18:30*).

Question Mark

A question mark is used in place of a period to show that the preceding sentence is a question:

> She actually volunteered to do it?

> Would you like another cup of coffee?

It is not used when the question is implied by indirect speech:

I asked you if you would like another cup of coffee.

A question mark may be used (typically in parentheses) to express doubt or uncertainty about a word or phrase immediately following or preceding it:

Jean Talon, born (?) 1625.

They were then seen boarding a bus (to Kingston?).

Exclamation Mark

An exclamation mark is used after an exclamatory word, phrase, or sentence expressing any of the following:

- Absurdity (*That's preposterous!*)
- Command or warning (*Watch out!*)
- Contempt or disgust (*Your hands are filthy!*)
- Emotion or pain (*I love this song! Ouch! That hurts!*)
- Enthusiasm (*I can't wait to see you!*)
- Wish or regret (*If only I could fly!*)
- Wonder, admiration, or surprise (*What a caring, compassionate person she is!*)

Apostrophe

The main use of an apostrophe is to indicate the possessive case, as in *Justine's book* or *the boys' mother*. It comes before the *s* in singular and plural nouns not ending in *s*, as in *the girl's costume* and *the women's costumes*. It comes after the *s* in plural nouns ending in *s*, as in *the girls' costumes*. In singular nouns ending in *s* practice differs between (for example) *Charles'* and *Charles's*; in some cases the shorter form is preferable for reasons of sound, as in *Xerxes' fleet* or in *Jesus' name*.

An apostrophe is used to indicate that a letter or series of letters has been removed to form a contraction: *we're, mustn't, Hallowe'en, o'clock*. It is sometimes used to form a plural of individual letters or numbers, although this use is diminishing. It is helpful in *dot your i's and cross your t's*, but unnecessary in *MPs* and *1940s*.

Quotation Marks

The main use of quotation marks is to indicate direct speech and quotations. Quotation marks are used at the beginning and end of quoted material:

She said, "I have something to tell you."

In standard North American practice, the closing quotation marks should come after any punctuation mark, whether or not it is part of the quoted matter:

They shouted, "Watch out!"

"Leave me," he said, "and never return."

They were described as "an unruly bunch."

Quotation marks may be placed around cited words and phrases:

> What does "integrated circuit" mean?

A quotation within a quotation is put in single quotation marks:

> "Have you any idea," he asked, "what 'integrated circuit' means?"

Note that in British practice, single quotation marks are often preferred, and the punctuation may be placed outside of the quotation marks when it does not belong to the quoted material:

> They were described as 'an unruly bunch'.

> 'Have you any idea', he asked, 'what "integrated circuit" means?'

Brackets (Parentheses)

The types of brackets used in normal punctuation are round brackets ( ), also known as parentheses, and square brackets [ ]. The main use of round brackets is to enclose explanations and extra information or comment:

> He was (and still is) a rebel.

> Congo (formerly Zaire).

> He spoke at length about his Weltanschauung (world view).

Brackets are also used to give references and citations:

> Wilfrid Laurier (1841–1919).

> A discussion of integrated circuits (see p. 38).

Brackets are used to enclose optional words:

> There are many (apparent) difficulties.

[In this example, the difficulties may or may not be only apparent.]

Square brackets are used less often. Their main use is to enclose extra information added by someone (normally an editor) other than the writer of the surrounding text:

> Robert walked in, and his sister [Sara] greeted him.

Square brackets are sometimes used to enclose extra information within text that is already in round brackets:

> Robert and Rebecca entered the room, and Sara greeted them. (Robert and Rebecca had concluded a three-week driving adventure [through Quebec] and had not seen Sara in some time.)

Dash

A single dash is used to indicate a pause, either to represent a hesitation in speech or to introduce an explanation of what comes before it:

> We must try to help—before it is too late.

A pair of dashes is used to enclose an aside or additional piece of information, like the use of commas as explained above, but forming a more distinct break:

He refused to tell anyone—least of all his wife—about that embarrassing moment during the medical exam.

A dash is sometimes used to indicate an omitted word or a portion of an omitted word, for example, a coarse or offensive word in reported speech:

"We were really p— off," he said.

It may also be used to sum up a list before carrying on with a sentence:

Chocolates, flowers, champagne—any of these would be appreciated.

Hyphen

The hyphen has two main functions: to link words to form longer words and com-pounds, and to mark the division of a word at the end of a line in print or writing.

The use of the hyphen to connect words to form compound words is diminishing in English. A hyphen is often retained to avoid awkward collisions of letters (as in *twist-tie*, *re-emerge*, or *miss-hit*) or to distinguish pairs of words (such as *re-sign* and *resign* or *re-creation* and *recreation*).

The hyphen serves to connect words that have a syntactic link, as in *soft-centred candies* and *French-speaking people*, where the reference is to candies with soft centres and people who speak French, rather than to soft candies with centres and French people who can speak (which would be the sense conveyed if the hyphens were omitted). It is also used to avoid more extreme kinds of ambiguity, as in *twenty-odd people*.

A particularly important use of the hyphen is to link compounds and phrases used attributively, as in *a well-known man* (but *the man is well known*), *water-cooler gossip* (but *gossip around the water cooler*), and *a sold-out show* (but *the show is sold out*).

A hyphen is often used to turn a phrasal verb into a noun:

She injured her shoulder in the *warm-up* before the game.

Notice, however, that while a hyphen is used in the noun, the verb is still spelled without a hyphen:

Stretching is a good way to *warm up* before a game.

A hyphen is also used to indicate a common second element in all but the last of a list, e.g., *two-*, *three-*, or *fourfold*.

The hyphen used to divide a word at the end of a line is a different matter because it is not a permanent feature of the spelling. The general principle to follow is to insert the hyphen where it will least distract the reader, usually at a syllable break.

Ellipsis

A sequence of three periods is used to mark an ellipsis, or omission, in a sequence of words, especially when forming an incomplete quotation. When the omission occurs at the end of a sentence, a fourth point is added as the period of the whole sentence:

He left the room, slammed the door . . . and went out.

The report said: "There are many issues to be considered, of which the most important are money, time, and personnel. . . . Let us consider personnel first."

Capitalization

A capital letter is used for the first letter of the word beginning a sentence:

> She decided not to come. Later she changed her mind.

A sentence contained in brackets within a larger sentence does not normally begin with a capital letter:

> I have written several essays (there are many to be written) and hope to finish them tomorrow.

However, in the following example, the sentence is a separate one, and so it does begin with a capital letter:

> We have more than one option. (You have said this often before.) For this reason, we should think carefully before acting.

A capital letter is used to begin sentences that form quoted speech:

> The assistant turned and replied, "We think it works."

The use of capital letters to distinguish proper nouns or names from ordinary words is subject to wide variation in practice. Some guidelines are offered here, but the most important criterion is consistency within a single piece of writing. Capital letters may be used for the following:

- The names of people and places (*Terry Fox, Prince Edward Island, Robson Street*)
- The names of languages, peoples, and words derived from these (*Inuktitut, Vietnamese, Quebecer, Englishwoman, Americanism*)
- The names of institutions and organizations (*the Crown, the Senate, the Department of Health, the National Museum of Natural Sciences, the Law Society of Upper Canada*)
- The names of religions and their adherents (*Judaism, Muslim, the United Church*)
- The names of months and days (*June, Monday, New Year's Day*)
- Nouns or abstract qualities personified (*a victim of Fate*)

Note that *the Anglican Church* is an institution, but *the Anglican church* is a building; a *Democrat* belongs to a political party, but a *democrat* simply supports democracy; *Northern Ireland* is a name with recognized status, but *northern England* is not.

A capital letter is used by convention in many names that are trademarks (*Xerox, Cineplex, Arborite*) or are otherwise associated with a particular manufacturer. Verbs derived from such proprietary terms are often not capitalized (*xeroxing, googled, skidooing*).

Capital letters are used in titles of courtesy or rank, including compound titles, when these directly precede a name (*the Right Honourable Lester B. Pearson, Dame Emma Albani, Brigadier General Daigle, Prime Minister Stephen Harper*). It is not necessary to capitalize a title when it is not placed directly before a name or when it is set off by commas (*an interview with Stephen Harper, prime minister of Canada; an interview with the prime minister, Stephen Harper*).

A capital letter is used for the name of a deity (*God, Father, Allah, Great Spirit*). However, the use of capitals in possessive adjectives and possessive pronouns (*in His name*) is now generally considered old-fashioned.

Capital letters are used for the first and other important words in titles of books, newspapers, plays, movies, and television programs (*The Merchant of Venice, Who Has Seen the Wind, The Vertical Mosaic, Hockey Night in Canada*).

Capital letters are used for historical events and periods (*the Dark Ages, the Enlightenment, the First World War*); also for geological time divisions but not for certain archaeological periods (*Devonian, Paleozoic,* but *neolithic*).

Capital letters are frequently used in abbreviations, with or without periods (*CTV, M.B.A.*).

A capital letter is used for a compass direction when abbreviated (*N, NE, NNE*) or when denoting a region (*cold weather in the North*).

Appendix C
The First Social Science Outline

Tentative Title of Term Paper

by

Student Name (if required, add student number)

Course Name, Number, and Section Number

Instructor

College or University

Date Submitted

The First Social Science Outline

General Topic: _____

Aim (what will be demonstrated) _____

_____

_____

Definition of Concepts (concepts from the aim that will be defined and their sources) _____

_____

_____

Organization of Arguments (the sequence of arguments) _____

1. _____
2. _____
3. _____
4. _____
5. _____

Presentation of Arguments (the points and evidence to support each point and their sources) _____

1. **Point:** _____

_____

Evidence: _____

_____

2. **Point:** _____

_____

Evidence: _____

_____

3. **Point:** _____

_____

_____

Evidence:

_____

_____

_____

4. **Point:**

_____

_____

Evidence:

_____

_____

5. **Point:**

_____

_____

Evidence:

_____

_____

_____

Conclusion (restate aim and how each argument supported the aim)

_____

_____

Aim (past tense):

_____

_____

1. Argument:

_____

_____

Supported aim:

_____

_____

2. Argument:

_____

_____

Supported aim:

_____

_____

3. Argument:

_____

_____

_____

Supported aim: _____

_____

4. Argument: _____

_____

Supported aim: _____

_____

5. Argument: _____

_____

Supported aim: _____

_____

References (APA style: list all books, periodicals, and other reference sources)

_____

_____

_____

_____

_____

_____

_____

_____

Appendix D

The Second Social Science Outline

Tentative Title of Term Paper

by

Student Name (if required, add student number)

Course Name, Number, and Section Number

Instructor

College or University

Date Submitted

The Second Social Science Outline

General Topic: _____

Aim (what will be demonstrated) _____

_____

_____

Definition of Concepts (concepts from the aim that will be defined and their sources) _____

_____

_____

Organization of Arguments (the sequence of headings or themes for groups of arguments: may contain subheadings and an individual argument)

1. Heading/Theme: _____
2. Heading/Theme: _____
3. Heading/Theme: _____
4. Heading/Theme: _____

Presentation of Arguments (the points and evidence to support each point and their sources)

1. **Point:** _____

Evidence: _____

2. **Point:** _____

Evidence: _____

3. **Point:** _____

Evidence: _____

_____

4. **Point:**

Evidence:

5. **Point:**

Evidence:

6. **Point:**

Evidence:

7. **Point:**

Evidence:

8. **Point:**

Evidence:

Conclusion (restate aim and then state how each heading or theme of arguments, including subheadings and any separate arguments, supported the aim)

Aim (past tense):

1. Heading/theme:

Supported aim:

2. Heading/theme:

Supported aim:

3. Heading/theme:

Supported aim:

4. Heading/theme:

Supported aim:

References (APA style: list all books, periodicals, and other reference sources)

_____

_____

_____

_____

_____

_____

_____

_____

_____

_____

_____

_____

_____

References

American Psychological Association. (2010). *Publication manual of the American Psychological Association.* (6th ed.). Washington, DC: Author.

American Psychological Association. (2007). *APA style guide to electronic references.* Washington, DC: Author. Available from http://www.apastyle.org.

Barnet, S., & Bedau, H. (2002). *Critical thinking, reading and writing.* Boston: Bedford/ St. Martin's.

Barnet, S., Stubbs, M., Bellanca, P., & Stimpson, P.G. (2003). *The practical guide to writing.* Toronto: Pearson.

Booth, W.C., Colomb, G.G., & Williams, J.M. (2008). *The craft of research.* Chicago: University of Chicago Press.

Corbett, E.P.J., & Connors, R.J. (1999). *Classical rhetoric for the modern student.* New York: Oxford University Press.

Cuba, L. (2002). *A short guide to writing about social science.* New York: Longman.

Dunn, S.D. (2004). *A short guide to writing about psychology.* New York: Pearson.

Ede, L. (2004). *Work in progress.* (6th ed.). Boston: Bedford/St. Martin's.

Fowler, H.R., Aaron, J.E., & McArthur, M. (2008). *The Little Brown handbook.* Toronto: Pearson/Longman.

Giarrusso, R. (Ed.). (2008). *A guide to writing sociology papers: The sociology writing group.* (6th ed.). New York: Worth.

Gibaldi, J. (2003). *MLA handbook for writers of research papers.* (5th ed.). New York: The Modern Language Association of America.

Hacker, D. (2006). *The Bedford handbook.* (7th ed.). Boston: Bedford/St. Martin's.

Kirszner, L.G., & Mandell, S.R. (2004). *Patterns for college writing.* (9th ed.). Boston: Bedford/St. Martin's.

Lester, J.D., Lester, J.D. Jr, & Mochnacz, P.I. (2003). *The essential guide to writing research papers.* Toronto: Longman.

Muth, F.M. (2006). *Researching and writing: A portable guide.* Boston: Bedford/ St. Martin's.

Northey, M. (2007). *Making sense: A student's guide to research and writing.* (5th ed.). Don Mills, ON: Oxford University Press.

Northey, M., & Tepperman, L. (1986). *Making sense in the social sciences.* Don Mills, ON: Oxford University Press.

Northey, M., & Timney, B. (2007). *Making sense: A student's guide to research and writing: Psychology and the life sciences.* (4th ed.). Don Mills, ON: Oxford University Press.

Norton, S., & Green, B. (2003). *Essay essentials.* Scarborough, ON: Thomson/Nelson.

Norton, S., & Green, B. (2006). *Essay essentials*. (4th ed.). Scarborough, ON: Thomson/ Nelson.

Odell, L., & Katz, S.M. (2006). *Writing in a visual age*. Boston: Bedford/St. Martin's.

Reinking, J.A., von der Osten, R., Cairns, S.A., & Fleming, R. (2007). *Strategies for successful writing: A rhetoric, research guide, reader, and handbook*. Upper Saddle River, NJ: Pearson.

Robertson, H. (1991). *The research essay*. Ottawa: Piperhill.

Roe, S.C., & den Ouden, P.H. (Eds.). (2003). *Designs for disciplines: An introduction to academic writing*. Toronto: Canadian Scholars' Press.

Sawers, N. (2002). *Ten steps to help you write better essays & term papers*. (3rd ed.). Edmonton, AB: NS Group.

Seyler, D.V. (1999). *Doing research*. Boston: McGraw-Hill College.

Stewart, K.L., & Allen, M. (2005). *Forms of writing*. Toronto: Pearson.

Stewart, K.L., Bullock, C.J., & Allen, M.E. (2004). *Essay writing for Canadian students*. Toronto: Pearson.

Szuchman, L.T. (2008). *Writing with style: APA style made easy*. (4th ed.) Belmont, CA: Thomson Wadsworth.

Turabian, K.L. (2007). *A manual for writers of research papers, theses, and dissertations*. (7th ed.). Chicago: University of Chicago Press.

Wood, N.V. (2001). *Writing argumentative essays*. Upper Saddle River, NJ: Prentice Hall.

Index